GCSE OCR Gateway
Additional Science
Foundation Workbook

This book is for anyone doing
GCSE OCR Gateway Additional Science at foundation level.
It covers everything you'll need for your year 11 exams.

It's full of **tricky questions**... each one designed to make you **sweat**
— because that's the only way you'll get any **better**.

There are questions to see **what facts** you know. There are questions
to see how well you can **apply those facts**. And there are questions
to see what you know about **how science works**.

It's also got some daft bits in to try and make the whole
experience at least vaguely entertaining for you.

What CGP is all about

Our sole aim here at CGP is to produce the highest
quality books — carefully written, immaculately presented
and dangerously close to being funny.

Then we work our socks off to get them
out to you — at the cheapest possible prices.

Contents

Module B3 — Living and Growing

Cells 1
Cells and DNA 2
Protein Synthesis and Mutations 3
Enzymes 5
Cell Division and Differentiation 7
Growth and Multi-cellular Organisms 8
Growth 9
Sexual Reproduction 10
Respiration 11
Respiration and Exercise 13
Functions of the Blood 14
Blood Vessels and the Heart 15
Selective Breeding 17
Genetic Engineering 18
Examples of Genetic Engineering 19
Cloning 20
Cloning Plants 21
Mixed Questions — Module B3 22

Module C3 — Chemical Economics

Atoms, Molecules and Compounds 24
Chemical Equations 26
Energy Transfer in Reactions 27
Measuring the Energy Content of Fuels 28
Chemical Reaction Rates 29
Collision Theory 30
Rate of Reaction Data 32
Reacting Masses 34
Calculating Masses in Reactions 36
Atom Economy 38
Percentage Yield 39
Chemical Production 41
Allotropes of Carbon 43
Mixed Questions — Module C3 45

Module P3 — Forces for Transport

Speed and Velocity 47
Speed and Distance 48
Speed and Acceleration 49
Forces 51
Friction 52
Weight and Terminal Speed 53
Forces and Acceleration 54
Stopping Distances 56
More on Stopping Distances 57
Momentum 58
Car Safety 60
Work Done and Power 61
Kinetic and Gravitational Potential Energy 63
Falling Objects and Roller Coasters 65
Fuel Consumption and Emissions 66
Fuels for Cars 67
Mixed Questions — Module P3 68

Module B4 — It's a Green World

Collecting Methods 71
Counting and Identifying Organisms 72
Estimating Population Sizes 73
Ecosystems and Distribution of Organisms 74
Distribution of Organisms 75
Biodiversity 76
Plants and Photosynthesis 77
More on Photosynthesis 78
Understanding Photosynthesis 79
Diffusion 80
Leaves and Diffusion 82
Leaves and Photosynthesis 83
Osmosis 84
Transport Systems in Plants 86
Water Flow Through Plants 87
Minerals Needed for Healthy Growth 89
More on Minerals 90
Decay 91
Preventing Decay 92
Intensive Farming 93
More on Farming 95
Mixed Questions — Module B4 96

Module C4 — The Periodic Table

The History of the Atom 98
Atoms 99
Elements and the Periodic Table 101
History of the Periodic Table 102
Electron Shells 103
Ionic Bonding 104
Ions and Ionic Compounds 105
Covalent Bonding 106
Group 1 — Alkali Metals 107
Group 7 — Halogens 109
Metals 111
Superconductors and Transition Metals 113
Thermal Decomposition and Precipitation 115
Water Purity 116
Testing Water Purity 117
Mixed Questions — Module C4 118

Module P4 — Radiation for Life

Static Electricity 120
More on Static Electricity 121
Uses of Static Electricity 122
Charge and Resistance 123
Plugs, Fuses and Power 125
Ultrasound Treatments and Scans 127
Radioactive Decay and Background Radiation 128
Radioactivity and Half-Life 129
Ionising Radiation 131
Medical Uses of Radiation 133
Other Uses of Radiation 134
Nuclear Power 135
Nuclear Fusion 137
Mixed Questions — Module P4 138

Published by CGP

Editors:
Katie Braid, Ben Fletcher, David Hickinson, Rachael Rogers, Helen Ronan, Hayley Thompson,
Karen Wells, Sarah Williams and Dawn Wright.

Contributors:
John Myers, Sidney Stringer Community School, Paul Warren.

ISBN: 978 1 84762 754 4

With thanks to Katherine Craig, Janet Cruse-Sawyer, Mark A Edwards, Mary Falkner,
Jamie Sinclair and Jane Towle for the proofreading.

With thanks to Jan Greenway, Laura Jakubowski and Laura Stoney for the copyright research.

Data used to draw graph on page 9, source — developed by the National Center for Health Statistics in collaboration with the National Center for Chronic Disease Prevention and Health Promotion (2000). http://www.cdc.gov/growthcharts

Data used to construct stopping distance diagram on page 57 from the Highway Code.
© Crown Copyright, reproduced under the terms of the Click-Use licence.

With thanks to the Deptartment of the Environment, Food and Rural Affairs for permission to use the data on page 93, reproduced under the terms of the Click-Use licence.

Every effort has been made to locate copyright holders and obtain permission to reproduce sources. For those sources where it has been difficult to trace the originator of the work, we would be grateful for information. If any copyright holder would like us to make an amendment to the acknowledgements, please notify us and we will gladly update the book at the next reprint. Thank you.

Groovy website: www.cgpbooks.co.uk

Printed by Elanders Ltd, Newcastle upon Tyne.
Jolly bits of clipart from CorelDRAW®
Based on the classic CGP style created by Richard Parsons.

Psst... photocopying this Workbook isn't allowed, even if you've got a CLA licence. Luckily, it's dead cheap, easy and quick to order more copies from CGP — just call us on 0870 750 1242. Phew!

Text, design, layout and original illustrations © Coordination Group Publications Ltd. (CGP) 2011
All rights reserved.

Module B3 — Living and Growing

Cells

Q1 Bacterial cells are different from plant and animal cells.

a) Circle three features of a typical plant cell that aren't seen in bacterial cells.

nucleus   cell membrane   cytoplasm   mitochondria   chloroplasts

b) Circle the correct word(s) to complete the following sentences.

i) Bacterial cells are **larger / smaller** than plant and animal cells.

ii) Bacterial cells are **simpler / more complex** than plant and animal cells.

Q2 Vacuoles and cell walls are features of plant cells.

Tick the boxes to show whether the following statements apply to the vacuole or cell wall. Some of the statements apply to both.

	Vacuole	Cell Wall
a) Contains cell sap.	☐	☐
b) Made of cellulose.	☐	☐
c) Provides the cell with support.	☐	☐

Q3 The diagram below shows a liver cell.

a) Label two mitochondria on the diagram.

b) Circle the process below which takes place in the mitochondria.

respiration   photosynthesis   protein synthesis

c) Explain why the liver cell has so many mitochondria.

....

....

d) Name one other type of cell that contains a large number of mitochondria.

....

Cells and DNA

Q1 Use the words below to complete the passage about making an **onion cell slide**.

| iodine | onion | cover slip | structures | slide | microscope | tweezers |

First, cut up an ...., then use .... to remove the slimy skin between the onion layers. Put this skin on a microscope ....
Then add a drop of .... solution — this will stain cell ....
Add a .... Now have a look at it under the ....

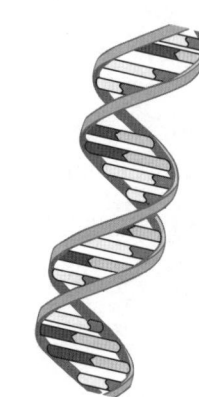

Q2 Circle the correct word(s) in each pair to complete the sentences.

a) **Proteins** / **chromosomes** are long, coiled molecules of DNA. They're found in the cell **nucleus** / **cytoplasm**.

b) DNA is divided into short sections called **amino acids** / **genes**.

c) DNA is a **double** / **single** helix made up of **four** / **six** different bases.

d) The strands in a DNA helix are joined together by **double** / **cross** links, which form between pairs of bases.

Q3 A **model** of **DNA** was first developed by two scientists called Watson and Crick. They used data that had been collected by other scientists.

a) Tick the box next to the statement below that correctly describes some of the data they used.

   1. X-ray data showing there was a single chain of DNA wound in a helix. ☐
   2. X-ray data showing there were two chains of DNA wound in a helix. ☐
   3. Infra-red data showing there were two chains of DNA wound in a helix. ☐

b) What other data did the two scientists use to develop their model?

....

Top Tips: There's quite a lot to get your head round with DNA — and a fair few tricky words you need to learn. Thank goodness some scientists found out so much about it though or else you'd never have that lovely, twisty helix to look at. Thank you Mr Watson. Thank you Mr Crick.

Module B3 — Living and Growing

Protein Synthesis and Mutations

Q1 Circle the correct word(s) in the pairs to complete the sentences below.

a) A gene is a section of DNA that codes for a **particular protein** / **cell structure**.

b) Each gene contains **a different** / **the same** sequence of bases.

c) Different cells produce the **same** / **different** proteins.

d) Different organisms produce the **same** / **different** proteins.

Q2 Genes control protein production using the **genetic code**.

a) What is the genetic code? Circle the correct answer below.

A set of coded instructions about how to make different proteins.

A set of coded instructions about how to make a new cell nucleus.

A set of coded instructions about how to make different carbohydrate molecules.

b) Apart from protein production, what else does the genetic code control? Give two answers below.

1. ....

2. ....

Q3 Proteins are made using a **copy** of the **code in genes**.

a) The diagram below shows a cell.

i) Where in the cell are **genes** found?

....

ii) Where in the cell are **proteins made**?

....

b) Explain why a gene needs to be copied to make proteins.

....

....

Module B3 — Living and Growing

Protein Synthesis and Mutations

Q4 a) What are **proteins** made of? Tick the correct box.

long chains of glucose molecules ☐   long chains of amino acids ☐

short chains of lipids ☐

b) Is the following statement **true** or **false**? Circle the correct answer.

"Proteins are not needed for cell growth or repair."   True   False

Q5 Draw lines to match each **protein** to its type and function.

protein	type	function
insulin	structural protein	transports oxygen around the body
haemoglobin	hormone	strengthens tissues
collagen	carrier molecule	controls blood sugar level

Q6 a) Tick the correct boxes to show whether the following statements are **true** or **false**.

	True	False
i) Mutations are always harmful.	☐	☐
ii) Mutations can happen spontaneously.	☐	☐
iii) Some mutations have no effect.	☐	☐
iv) Mutations never lead to the production of different proteins.	☐	☐
v) Mutations are changes to the cell cytoplasm.	☐	☐

Ben's pet ant had been mute since the unfortunate squishing incident.

b) Give two things that can cause mutations to happen more often.

1. ....

2. ....

Top Tips: Sadly mutations sin the real world are nowhere near as great as the ones in films and comics — no mutation has ever given anyone x-ray vision or the ability to fly. Make sure you know how mutations are caused and the sorts of results they really have.

Module B3 — Living and Growing

Enzymes

Q1 Tick the boxes to show whether the sentences are **true** or **false**.

		True	False
a)	Enzymes slow down chemical reactions in living cells.	☐	☐
b)	The reactions involved in photosynthesis are controlled by enzymes.	☐	☐
c)	Enzymes don't control reactions involved with protein synthesis.	☐	☐
d)	Enzymes are proteins.	☐	☐

Q2 This question is all about **how enzymes work**.

a) Enzymes usually only work with **one substrate**. What's the scientific way of saying this? Tick the correct answer below.

- Enzymes are differentiated from their substrate. ☐
- Enzymes mutate to match their substrate. ☐
- Enzymes have a high specificity for their substrate. ☐

b) For a reaction to be catalysed by an enzyme, the substrate needs to fit into the enzyme. What's this called? Circle the correct answer below.

- The lock and key mechanism.
- The hand in hand mechanism.
- The perfect shape mechanism.

c) Name the part of the enzyme that joins onto its substrate.

....

Q3 In the space provided, draw a labelled diagram to show how an enzyme's shape allows it to break substances down.

Module B3 — Living and Growing

Enzymes

Q4 This graph shows the results from an investigation into the effect of **temperature** on the rate of an **enzyme** catalysed reaction.

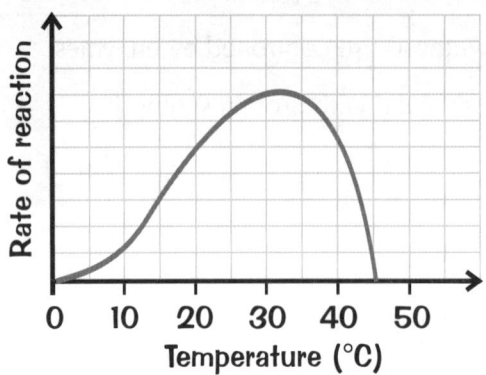

a) i) What does the term '**optimum temperature**' mean? Underline the correct answer below.

The highest temperature at which an enzyme can work.

The temperature at which an enzyme works best.

ii) What is the optimum temperature for this enzyme? ....

b) What happens to the **rate of reaction** when the temperature gets hotter than the optimum temperature?

....

Q5 Stuart has a sample of an enzyme and he is trying to find out what its **optimum pH** is. Stuart tests the enzyme by **timing** how long it takes to break down a substance at different pH levels. The results of Stuart's experiment are shown in the table below.

pH	time taken for reaction in seconds
2	101
4	83
6	17
8	76
10	99
12	102

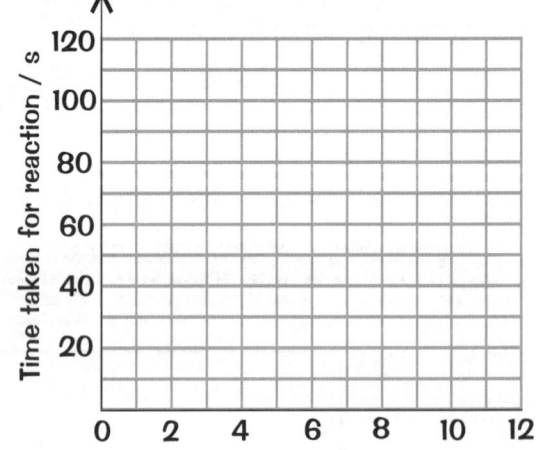

a) On the grid to the right draw a line graph of the results of the experiment.

b) What is the **optimum** pH for the enzyme?

....

c) What happens to the rate of reaction when the pH is **lower** than the optimum?

....

Module B3 — Living and Growing

Cell Division and Differentiation

Q1 New cells for growth are produced by cell division.

a) Circle the type of cell division that makes new cells for growth.

   differentiation   mitosis   meiosis   specialisation

b) What else is this type of cell division used for? Circle **three** correct answers below.

   asexual reproduction   repairing damaged tissues   making gametes   replacing worn out cells

Q2 Complete the passage below using some of the words provided.

| replicates | full amount | halved | different | identical | copied | changes |

Mitosis makes two new cells that are genetically ....

Every time a cell divides by mitosis the chromosomes have to be ....

So before cell division begins, DNA ....

This is so that the new cells have the .... of DNA.

Q3 Most cells in your body are **specialised** for a particular job. Others are **undifferentiated**.

a) i) What are **undifferentiated cells** called? Circle the correct answer below.

   clones   sex cells   stem cells

ii) What can undifferentiated cells develop into?

....

b) Name the process called by which cells become specialised.

....

Q4 People have **different opinions** when it comes to **stem cell research**.

a) Give one argument **in favour** of stem cell research.

....

b) Give one argument **against** stem cell research.

....

Module B3 — Living and Growing

Growth and Multi-cellular Organisms

Q1 Which of the following are involved in **growth**? Circle **two** correct answers.

fertilisation   cell division   mutation   cell specialisation

Q2 Using the labels below, complete the table to show the **differences** between **plant** and **animal** growth. Two have already been done for you.

~~Grow only when they're young.~~   All parts of the organism grow.   ~~Grow throughout their lives.~~

Growth by cell division only happens in the meristems.

Don't lose the ability to differentiate.   All growth happens by cell division.

Lose the ability to differentiate at an early stage.   Growth in height is by cell enlargement.

ANIMALS	PLANTS
Grow only when they're young.	Grow throughout their lives.

Q3 Some organisms are **unicellular** whereas others have evolved to be **multi-cellular**.

a) i) What is a **unicellular** organism?

....

ii) What is a **multi-cellular** organism?

....

b) Give three **advantages** of being multi-cellular compared to being unicellular.

1. ....

2. ....

3. ....

Module B3 — Living and Growing

Growth

Q1 Growth can be measure as an increase in height.

a) What else can growth be measured as an increase in? Write down two answers.

1. ....

2. ....

b) What is the **best** measure of growth in plants and animals?

....

Q2 The graph is an example of a **human growth curve**. It shows three different phases of growth.

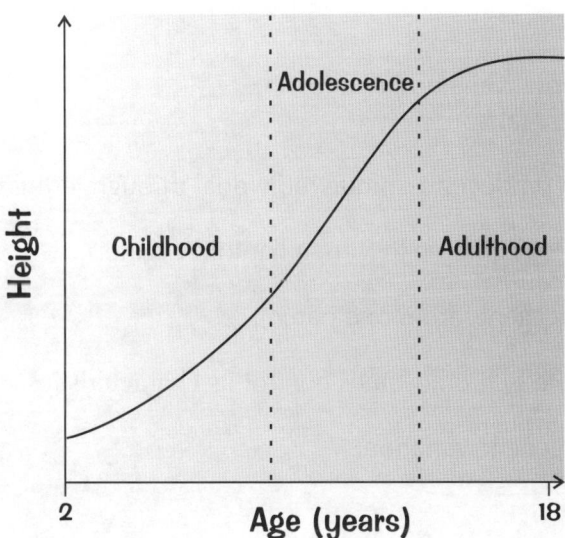

a) Look at the growth curve above. Circle the correct description of growth during **childhood**.

There is no growth during childhood.   Growth is rapid at first then slows down.

Growth is steady throughout childhood.

b) i) During which phase on this growth curve is growth **fastest**?

....

ii) Name another phase of **rapid human growth**, which is not shown on this growth curve.

....

Module B3 — Living and Growing

Sexual Reproduction

Q1 Choose from the following words to complete the passage below.

> haploid   meiosis   sperm   copies
> pairs   half   diploid   egg

Gametes are the .... and .... cells. They're formed by a process called .... In mammals, all body cells are .... This means they contain two .... of each chromosome in matching .... However gametes are ...., which means they contain .... the number of chromosomes as body cells.

Q2 Tick the boxes to show whether the following statements are **true** or **false**.

                                                                                     True   False
a) Sexual reproduction produces a unique individual through fertilisation.   ☐   ☐
b) At fertilisation gametes combine to form a haploid zygote.   ☐   ☐
c) A zygote gets all of its genes from one parent.   ☐   ☐
d) The genes on a zygote's chromosomes control its characteristics.   ☐   ☐
e) Fertilisation creates genetic variation.   ☐   ☐

The name is Goat. Zy Goat.

Q3 a) Circle the correct words to complete the sentence below.

Sperm cells are produced in **small** / **large** numbers to **increase** / **decrease** the chance of fertilisation.

b) **Sperm** are adapted to fertilising egg cells. Explain how the following features make sperm cells adapted to their function:

i) many mitochondria.

....

ii) an acrosome.

....

Module B3 — Living and Growing

Respiration

Q1 **Respiration** releases the energy needed for **all life processes** in plants and animals. Give three examples of life processes that need energy from respiration.

1. ....

2. ....

3. ....

Q2 a) Circle the correct word equation for **aerobic respiration**.

protein + oxygen → carbon dioxide + water (+ energy)

glucose + oxygen → carbon dioxide + water (+ energy)

glucose + carbon dioxide → oxygen + water (+ energy)

b) Complete the **chemical equation** below for **aerobic respiration**:

.... + $6O_2$ → $6CO_2$ + ... (+ ....)

Q3 Humans can respire **anaerobically**.

a) When would someone use anaerobic respiration? Circle the correct answer below.

| During gentle exercise. | During hard exercise. | When they're asleep. |

b) Give two **disadvantages** of **anaerobic** respiration.

1. ....

....

2. ....

....

c) Write the **word equation** for anaerobic respiration in humans.

.... → .... (+ ....)

Module B3 — Living and Growing

Respiration

Q4 Jim takes part in a race. The **graph** below shows Jim's **oxygen consumption** before, during and after the race.

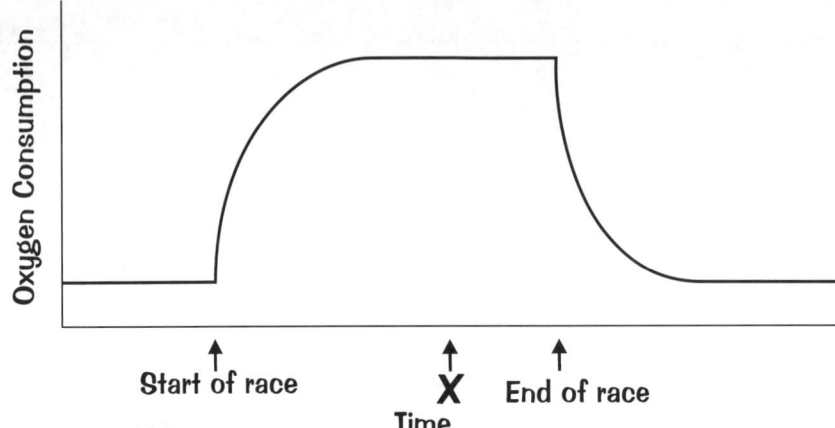

a) i) Describe what happens to Jim's oxygen consumption **during** the race.

....

ii) Describe what happens to Jim's oxygen consumption **after** the race.

....

b) Complete the sentence below using the correct word from the list.

As Jim's oxygen consumption increases, his respiration rate ....

increases   stays the same   decreases

c) At what point in the race would Jim's **carbon dioxide production** be highest? Circle the correct answer.

At the very start of the race.   In the middle of the race.

A little while after the race.

d) Circle the answer which best describes the respiration taking place at point **X** on the graph.

Aerobic respiration only.   Anaerobic and aerobic respiration.

Anaerobic respiration only.

e) Jim's leg muscles are painful after the race. Suggest what substance caused the pain.

....

Top Tips: Get to grips with what happens to oxygen consumption and carbon dioxide production during respiration and hey presto — you'll be a respiration expert in no time. Or at least you'll know enough to answer questions on it in the exam.

Module B3 — Living and Growing

Respiration and Exercise

Q1 Judy decided to measure the **respiratory quotient** of two mice. Her data is presented in the table below.

	Oxygen Used (cm³)	Carbon Dioxide Produced (cm³)
Mouse A	26.5	31.8
Mouse B	29.1	26.2

$$RQ = \frac{\text{Amount of } CO_2 \text{ produced}}{\text{Amount of } O_2 \text{ used}}$$

Calculate the respiratory quotient of each mouse using the formula given above.

a) Mouse A: ....

b) Mouse B: ....

Q2 During exercise **breathing rate** and **heart rate** increase. Circle the **two** sentences below that explain why this happens.

| So oxygen can be removed from the body more quickly. | So carbon dioxide can be removed from the body more quickly. | So carbon dioxide can be delivered to the heart more quickly. | So oxygen and glucose can be delivered to the muscles more quickly. |

Q3 Roy wants to find out which of his friends **recovers** the quickest after exercise. Roy tests each of his friends separately. He measures their **pulse rates**, then asks them to **run**. After they've finished running he measures their pulse rates at regular intervals until they have returned to normal.

The results are shown in the table below.

	Pulse rate before exercise / beats per minute	Pulse rate 60 s after end of exercise / beats per minute	Pulse rate 120 s after end of exercise / beats per minute	Pulse rate 180 s after end of exercise / beats per minute
Jim	60	62	60	60
Saeed	72	90	82	77
Bonnie	75	95	85	75

a) Describe how you could take someone's pulse.

....

....

b) Which of his friends recovers the quickest?

....

Think about how long it takes their pulse rates to return to normal.

Module B3 — Living and Growing

Functions of the Blood

Q1 Tick the correct boxes to show whether these statements are **true** or **false**.

		True	False
a)	The function of red blood cells is to fight germs.	☐	☐
b)	White blood cells help to clot blood.	☐	☐
c)	Platelets help to clot blood.	☐	☐
d)	The liquid part of blood is called urine.	☐	☐

Q2 a) Tick the sentence that best describes the **function** of plasma.

☐ To carry things that need transporting around the body.

☐ To carry things that need transporting in and out of red blood cells.

☐ To carry things that need transporting through the digestive tract.

b) Which of the following is **not** carried by the plasma? Circle the correct answer.

glucose and amino acids   oxygen   antibodies   hormones   waste products like carbon dioxide

Q3 Use the words below to complete the passage about the structure of **red blood cells**.

small   biconcave   haemoglobin
large   nucleus   capillaries

Red blood cells are .... in shape. This means they have a .... surface area for absorbing oxygen.

They are very .... in size so they can easily pass through the .... Red blood cells have no ....

They contain .... which combines with oxygen.

Module B3 — Living and Growing

Blood Vessels and the Heart

Q1 Draw lines to match each of the blood vessels below with its correct job.

vein — involved in the exchange of materials at the tissues

artery — takes blood away from the heart

capillary — takes blood to the heart

Q2 Circle the correct word(s) in each pair to complete the sentences below.

a) The blood pressure in the **arteries** / **veins** is higher than in the **arteries** / **veins**.

b) The **right** / **left** side of the heart pumps blood to the lungs.

c) The **right** / **left** side of the heart pumps blood to the rest of the body.

Q3 The diagram below shows the human **heart**, as seen from the front. Three labels have been done for you. Complete the remaining labels **a)** to **h)**.

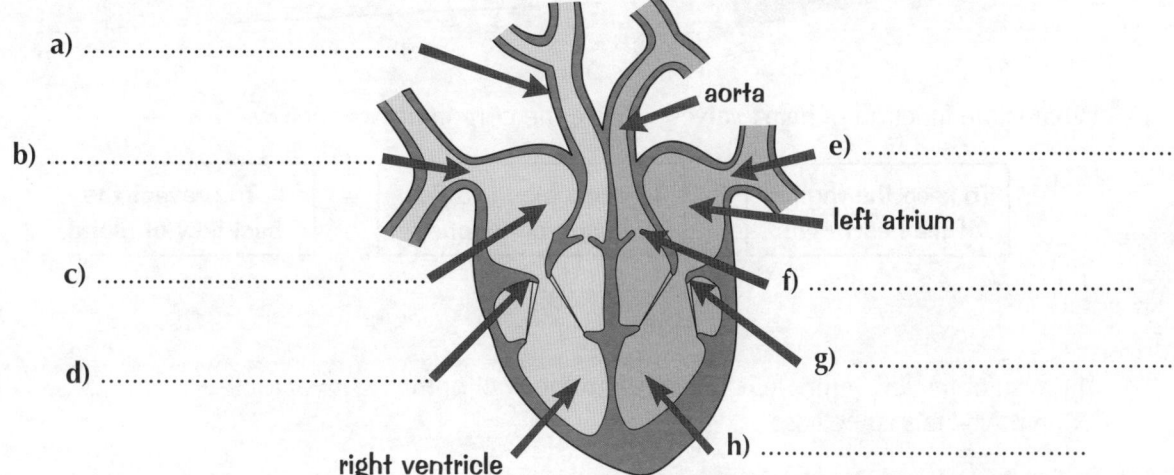

a) ....
b) ....
c) ....
d) ....
e) ....
f) ....
g) ....
h) ....

Labelled: aorta, left atrium, right ventricle

Top Tips: The heart can seem quite complicated at first. Try to learn what the heart looks like and where everything is and it'll be much easier to understand what's going on.

Module B3 — Living and Growing

Blood Vessels and the Heart

Q4 Write either **right** or **left** in the spaces to complete each of the following sentences.

a) The .... atrium of the heart receives deoxygenated blood.

b) The .... ventricle pumps deoxygenated blood to the lungs.

c) The .... atrium of the heart receives oxygenated blood from the lungs.

d) The .... ventricle pumps oxygenated blood to the rest of the body.

Q5 a) Circle the correct word in each pair to complete the sentence below.

Blood flows through the heart from areas of **high** / **low** pressure to areas of **high** / **low** pressure.

b) Draw lines to match each of the blood vessels to its function. One's been done for you.

- pulmonary vein — carries blood into the right atrium
- aorta — carries blood into the left atrium
- pulmonary artery — carries blood out of the left ventricle
- vena cava — carries blood out of the right ventricle

c) What is the function of **heart valves**? Circle the correct answer below.

- To keep the rhythm of the heart right.
- To allow blood to flow in any direction.
- To prevent the backflow of blood.

Q6 The wall of the left ventricle is **thicker** than the wall of the right ventricle. Explain why this is the case.

....

....

....

Module B3 — Living and Growing

Selective Breeding

Q1 Penelope has a friend with a variety of smiley tomato plants. She wants her own plant with really **big fruit**.

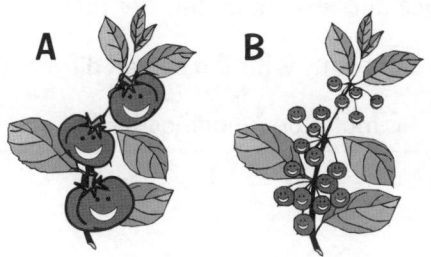

a) Circle the combination of plants she should breed together to get plants with the biggest possible fruit.

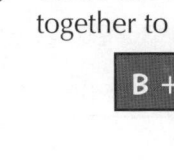 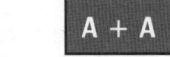

b) Number the following statements **1** to **5** to show how Penelope could gradually produce plants with bigger and bigger fruit.

☐ Breed them with each other.

☐ Select the best of the offspring.

☐ Continue the process over several generations.

☐ Breed them with each other.

☐ Select plants with the biggest tomatoes.

c) Suggest **one** problem that selective breeding might cause in the tomatoes.

....

Q2 The graph shows the **average milk yield** for a population of cows over three generations. The three generations of cows were all kept in the same conditions.

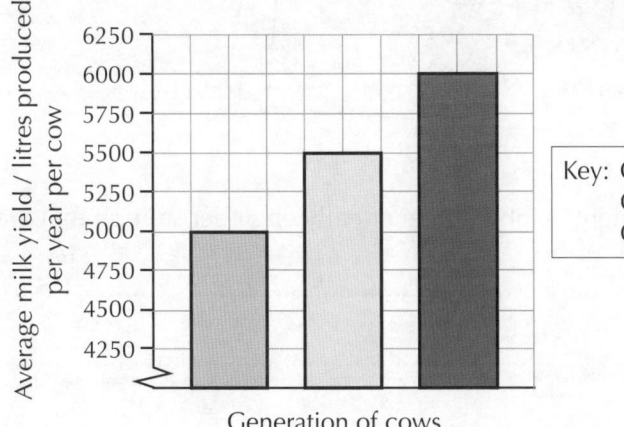

a) What has happened to the average milk yield over the three generations of cows?

....

b) What might have caused the change in average milk yield over the three generations?

....

Module B3 — Living and Growing

Genetic Engineering

Q1 Complete the sentences by circling the correct word(s) in each pair.

> In genetic engineering scientists select **genes** / **enzymes** and artificially transfer them from one **dead** / **living** organism to another. This produces organisms with **the same** / **different** characteristics. Another name for this process is genetic **mutation** / **modification**.

Q2 a) Give **one advantage** of genetic engineering.

....

b) Give **one risk** involved in genetic engineering.

....

Q3 James is a fishmonger. He thinks he could sell more salmon if only they were a bit more like trout.

a) Look at the notes he has made about the fish.
Suggest **three** characteristics of trout James might like the salmon to have.

Think about which characteristics are most useful.

Salmon
Slow growing
Grow to around 20 kg
Feed on flies
Often killed by sea lice
Swim long distances

Trout
Fast growing
Grow to around 15 kg
Feed on flies
Resistant to sea lice
Produce lots of offspring

1. ....
2. ....
3. ....

b) Describe how scientists might be able to genetically engineer salmon that are more like trout.

....

....

Q4 Some people are **worried** about the ethical issues involved in genetic engineering.
Explain **one** reason why this is.

....

....

Module B3 — Living and Growing

Examples of Genetic Engineering

Q1 **Genetic engineering** has lots of uses.

a) Use the words in the box to fill in the blank spaces in the passage below.

vitamin A	rice	carrot	rice
In some parts of the world rice is a main source of food. Scientists have taken the gene that controls beta-carotene production in .... plants and put it into .... plants. When humans eat the .... they can convert the beta-carotene into			

b) i) How could genetic engineering be used to make plants **resistant to herbicides**?

....

....

ii) Other than herbicides, give two examples of things plants can be made resistant to.

1. ....

2. ....

c) Describe how genetic engineering has affected the production of **human insulin**.

....

....

Q2 a) What does **gene therapy** involve? Tick the box next to the correct answer.

☐ Using a person's genes for research once they have died.

☐ Changing a person's genes in an attempt to cure a genetic disorder.

☐ Altering the genes of a plant or animal to improve agricultural yields.

b) Is the following statement **true** or **false**? Circle the correct answer.

'There are thousands of people alive in the UK today who have been helped by gene therapy.'

True   False

Top Tips: Genetic engineering is nearly always in the news these days. Scientists are able to change all sorts of organisms so they're more beneficial to us. Hmm, I wonder when they'll develop a cow that produces strawberry flavoured milk...

Module B3 — Living and Growing

Cloning

Q1 It's possible to **clone animals**.

a) What are clones? Underline the correct answer.

Organisms that have very similar genes.

Organisms that are genetically identical copies of each other.

Organisms that look identical to each other but have different genes.

b) Circle the correct word in each pair to complete the sentences below.

i) Cloning is an example of **asexual** / **sexual** reproduction.

ii) Identical twins are **naturally** / **artificially** occurring clones.

iii) The first mammal to be cloned was **Dotty** / **Dolly** the sheep.

iv) This sheep was produced by a process called **genetic** / **nuclear** transfer.

c) Choose from some of the following words to complete the sentence below.

mitochondria   a body   an egg   nucleus

An animal can be cloned by putting the ....
from .... cell into .... cell.

Q2 a) Which statement describes a possible **use of cloning**? Tick the box.

☐ Producing lots of cows that all have a high milk yield.

☐ Producing a few chickens that all lay different sized eggs.

b) Describe **one** other possible use of cloning.

....

....

Q3 Describe **one ethical** issue involved in **cloning humans**.

....

....

....

Module B3 — Living and Growing

Cloning Plants

Q1 a) Circle the correct words to complete the passage below.

> Some plants can reproduce **asexually / sexually** by mitosis. This means they produce **clones / similar copies** of themselves. The involvement of another plant is **needed / not needed**. Strawberry plants produce **runners / tubers**. These are shoots that grow over the ground and form leaves and roots of their own. Potato plants can grow swollen underground organs called **runners / tubers**.

b) Name **one** other plant that reproduces asexually by producing **runners**.

....

Q2 Rachel has a flowering plant with especially attractive characteristics. She decides to grow more plants by taking **cuttings**.

a) By growing cuttings of her plant will Rachel be producing **clones**? ....

b) Describe how Rachel should take a cutting of the plant.

....

....

c) Circle another technique that can be used to clone plants.

tissue culture   stem replication   genetic planting

Q3 Alfie is setting up a banana farm and is trying to decide whether or not to use **cloned** plants.

a) Tick **two advantages** of Alfie choosing cloned plants.

- [ ] He'll have bananas with a lot of genetic variation.
- [ ] He'll know what the bananas are going to look like before they've even grown.
- [ ] He can combine the best characteristics from different banana plants.
- [ ] He'll be able to mass produce his plants which may have been difficult to do from seeds.

b) Suggest **one disadvantage** of using cloned plants.

....

....

Module B3 — Living and Growing

Mixed Questions — Module B3

Q1 Humans can respire **aerobically** and **anaerobically**.

a) Tick the boxes to show whether the statements are **true** or **false**.

	True	False
i) Respiration only releases energy for one or two life processes.	☐	☐
ii) Respiration only happens in animals.	☐	☐
iii) Respiration is controlled by enzymes.	☐	☐
iv) Respiration takes place in the mitochondria.	☐	☐

b) Circle the correct word in each pair to complete the following sentences about **anaerobic respiration** in humans.

　i) Anaerobic respiration is respiration without **glucose / oxygen**.

　ii) Anaerobic respiration produces **lactic acid / water**.

　iii) **Less / More** energy is released per glucose molecule during anaerobic respiration than during aerobic respiration.

Q2 Draw lines to match each part of the **blood** to its function.

red blood cells	transports different substances around the body
white blood cells	help blood to clot
platelets	transport oxygen around the body
plasma	help to fight disease

Q3 Plants and animals have many similarities and differences.

a) Tick the boxes to say whether the following statements apply to **plants**, **animals** or **both**.

	Plants	Animals	Both
i) Cells have a vacuole.	☐	☐	☐
ii) Cells have a nucleus.	☐	☐	☐
iii) Organism gains height by cell enlargement.	☐	☐	☐
iv) Organism stops growing when a particular size is reached.	☐	☐	☐
v) Organism can be genetically engineered.	☐	☐	☐

b) Give two ways in which a **bacterial cell** is different from a plant or animal cell.

1. ....

2. ....

Module B3 — Living and Growing

Mixed Questions — Module B3

Q4 The diagram shows part of the **circulatory system**.

a) Name the blood vessels labelled W, X, Y and Z.

W ....

X ....

Y ....

Z ....

b) Which type of blood vessel contains valves?

....

Q5 Lucy has been revising for her exam by writing down the definitions of some important words. Unfortunately her paper has been torn. Fill in the missing words for the definitions on Lucy's paper. Choose words from the box.

Definitions

A short section of DNA that controls some of the characteristics of an organism = ...

A long chain of amino acids needed for cell growth and repair = ...

A molecule that can speed up a chemical reaction = ...

Enzyme Gamete Protein DNA Gene

Q6 Humans can have some control over an organism's **characteristics**.

a) Fill in the blanks using the words from the box.

generations	bred	yields	offspring	characteristics

In selective breeding organisms with the desired .... are selected and then .... together. The best .... are then selected to breed together. This process is repeated over several ....

In farming, selective breeding can be used to improve agricultural ....

b) Name **one** other method that humans can use to control an organism's characteristics.

....

Module B3 — Living and Growing

Atoms, Molecules and Compounds

Q1 Substances are made up of **atoms**.

a) Complete the missing label on this diagram of an atom. ....

b) State whether the following statement is **true** or **false**.

Electrons are positively charged.

....

Q2 Circle the correct words from each pair to complete the sentences below.

a) If an atom **gains** / **loses** electrons it becomes a positive ion.

b) If an atom **gains** / **loses** electrons it becomes a negative ion.

c) When a negative ion is attracted to a positive ion they form **a covalent** / **an ionic** bond.

Q3 The diagram on the right shows a molecule of **butane**.

Fill in the gaps in the following paragraph using words from the list below.

| atoms | covalent | electrons |

Butane is a compound made up of two different sorts of ....

They join together because .... are shared between them.

This means .... bonds are formed.

Q4 Chemical **formulas** can tell you what type of substance something is.

a) Circle the formula below that shows an **ion**.

CO_2 H_2O Cl^- H_2

b) Circle the formula below that shows a **molecule**.

Cl H_2O Ca^{2+} O

c) Circle the formula below that shows an **atom**.

H_2 O_2 C Ca^{2+}

d) Circle the formula below that shows an **element**.

H_2 $NaCl$ CO_2 $CaCO_3$

e) Circle the formula below that shows a **compound**.

H^+ H_2O O_2 Na^+

Atoms, Molecules and Compounds

Q5 The **displayed** formula for **propanol** is shown on the right.

a) What is the **molecular** formula of propanol? ....

b) How many **carbon** atoms does a molecule of propanol contain?

....

c) How many atoms does a molecule of propanol contain **in total**?

....

Q6 **Chemical formulas** are used to show elements and compounds.

a) Write the names of the elements and compounds listed below.

i) $CaCO_3$ ....   ii) H_2 ....

iii) HCl ....

b) State how many **hydrogen** atoms there are in the compounds below.

i) H_2SO_4 ....   ii) CH_3CH_2COOH ....

Q7 This is the molecular formula of **pentane**.

$$CH_3(CH_2)_3CH_3$$

a) State the total number of atoms in pentane.

....

b) In a molecule of pentane, what is the total number of atoms of:

i) carbon? ....   ii) hydrogen? ....

Q8 Complete the table to show the **molecular formulas** of water, carbon dioxide and ammonia.

NAME	DISPLAYED FORMULA	MOLECULAR FORMULA
WATER	H–O–H	a)
CARBON DIOXIDE	O=C=O	b)
AMMONIA	H–N(–H)–H	c)

Module C3 — Chemical Economics

Chemical Equations

Q1 Complete the table below to show the **reactants** and the **products** in each of the equations.

Equation	Reactants	Products
$Ca + 2H_2O \rightarrow Ca(OH)_2 + H_2$		
hydrogen peroxide $\rightarrow$ water + oxygen		
$2Mg + O_2 \rightarrow 2MgO$		

Q2 This is the **symbol equation** for burning methane in air:

$$CH_4 + 2O_2 \rightarrow CO_2 + 2H_2O$$

a) How many C, H and O atoms are shown on the **left-hand** side of the equation?

C .... H .... O ....

b) How many C, H and O atoms are shown on the **right-hand** side of the equation?

C .... H .... O ....

c) Is this equation balanced? Explain your answer.

....

Q3 Tick the correct boxes to show which of the following equations are **balanced** correctly.

	Correctly balanced	Incorrectly balanced
a) $2Na + Cl_2 \rightarrow 2NaCl$	☐	☐
b) $Li + 2H_2O \rightarrow LiOH + H_2$	☐	☐
c) $H_2SO_4 + ZnO \rightarrow ZnSO_4 + H_2O$	☐	☐
d) $Cl_2 + 2KI \rightarrow I_2 + KCl$	☐	☐
e) $CuCO_3 \rightarrow CuO + CO_2$	☐	☐

$Fe_2O_3 + 3CO \rightarrow 2Fe + 3CO_2$

Top Tip: Balancing equations isn't too bad — count the number of each type of atom on the left side and then on the right side. If each atom has the same number on both sides, then it's balanced.

Module C3 — Chemical Economics

Energy Transfer in Reactions

Q1 Use the words from the box to **complete** the passage below. Use each word only once.

> endothermic   exothermic   an increase   a decrease
>
> All chemical reactions involve changes in energy.
>
> In .... reactions, heat energy is given out to the surroundings.
>
> A thermometer will show .... in temperature.
>
> In .... reactions, heat energy is taken in from the surroundings.
>
> A thermometer will show .... in temperature.

Q2 Fiz investigated the **temperature change** during a reaction. She recorded the temperature of the reaction mixture **every 15 seconds** for **two minutes**.

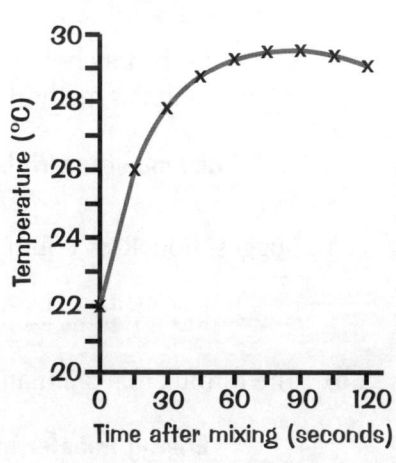

Fiz plotted her results on the graph shown.

a) State whether the temperature increased or decreased during the reaction.

....

b) Circle the word below that describes the reaction in this experiment.

    endothermic   exothermic

Q3 **Circle** the correct words to complete each of the sentences below.

a) Bond breaking is an **exothermic / endothermic** process.

b) Bond making is an **exothermic / endothermic** process.

Q4 Label each of the reactions below as **exothermic** or **endothermic**.

a) 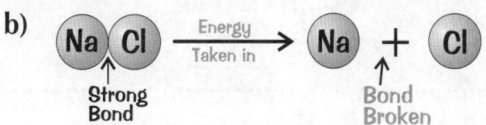   ....

b) Na Cl —Energy Taken in→ Na + Cl
  Strong Bond   Bond Broken   ....

Module C3 — Chemical Economics

Measuring the Energy Content of Fuels

Q1 Ross wants to compare the **energy content** of petrol and a different fuel, fuel X. He uses a calorimetric method

a) On the right, label the diagram to show the equipment Ross uses.

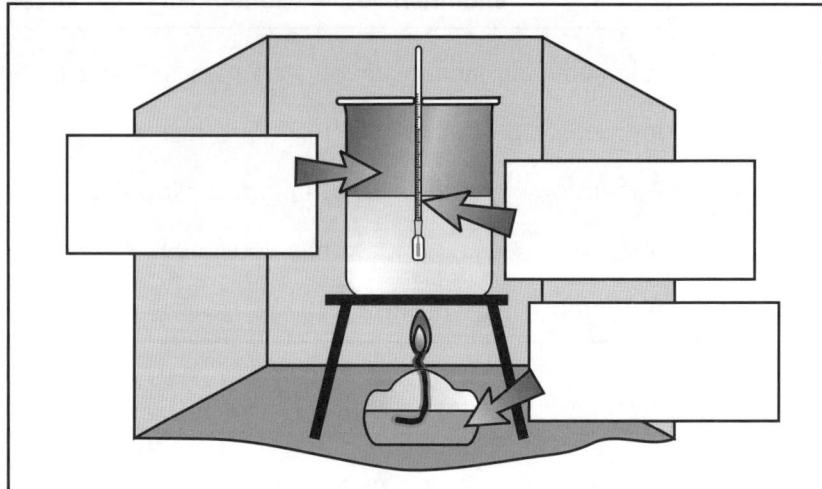

b) Circle the **factors** below that Ross needs to keep the same when using this method to make sure it's a fair test.

distance of spirit burner to can   **type of fuel**   **mass of water used**

c) Suggest how Ross could make sure that his results were **reliable**.

....

d) The formula for calculating the energy transferred is:

Energy transferred (J) = mass of water (g) × 4.2 × change in temperature (°C)

i) He finds that the petrol raises the temperature of **50 g** of water by **30.5 °C**. Calculate the energy transferred to the water by the petrol.

....

....

ii) Burning fuel X raises the temperature of **50 g** of water by **27 °C**. Calculate the energy transferred to the water by fuel X.

....

....

e) Ross tests two more fuels.

Fuel Y released 5960 J and fuel Z released 5520 J.

Explain whether fuel Y or fuel Z would make the better fuel.

....

....

Chemical Reaction Rates

Q1 Reactions can happen at different speeds.

Match these common chemical reactions to the **speed** at which they happen.

- a firework going off
- hair being dyed
- an apple rotting

- SLOW (hours or longer)
- MODERATE SPEED (minutes)
- FAST (seconds or shorter)

- iron rusting
- a match burning
- oil paint drying

Q2 Tick the boxes to show whether the following statements are **true** or **false**.

True False

a) A chemical reaction takes place when particles collide. ☐ ☐

b) The more collisions, the slower the rate of reaction. ☐ ☐

c) Rate of reaction measures how much product is made in a certain amount of time. ☐ ☐

Q3 Joe measured the **rate** of a reaction. He added 1 g of **calcium carbonate powder** to 100 cm³ of **dilute hydrochloric acid**. The equation for the reaction that took place is shown below.

$$CaCO_3(s) + 2HCl(aq) \rightarrow CaCl_2(aq) + CO_2(g) + H_2O(l)$$

a) Joe used the equipment shown to measure the amount of gas given off during the experiment. Complete the diagram by labelling the equipment.

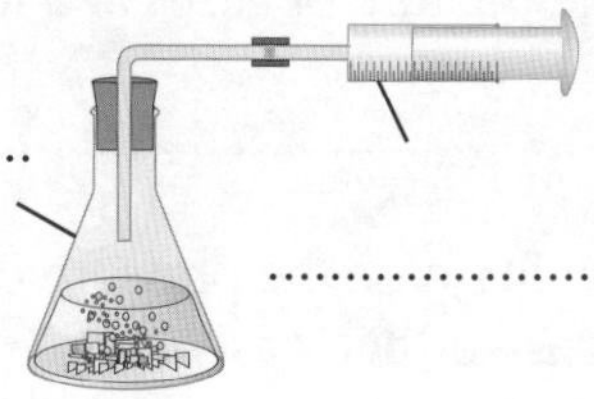

b) After two minutes there was still some powder left at the bottom of the flask, but no more gas was produced.

  i) Circle the reactant that is the limiting reactant.   **CaCO₃**   **HCl**

  ii) Explain why the reaction stopped. ....

....

c) Joe is going to repeat the experiment. This time he plans to add half as much of the limiting reactant. Circle the amount of calcium chloride you think will be produced. Explain your answer.

      half as much   the same amount   twice as much

....

....

Module C3 — Chemical Economics

Collision Theory

Q1 Why do we usually use **catalysts**? Circle the correct letter.

A   To stop reactions   B   To speed up reactions

C   To slow down reactions   D   To make reactions reversible

Q2 Draw lines to match up the changes with their effects on the particles.

- increasing the temperature — makes the particles move faster, so they collide more often
- decreasing the concentration — means more of a solid reactant will be able to react with the other reactant
- increasing the surface area — means fewer particles of reactants are present in a given volume, so they'll collide less often

Q3 Below are two diagrams showing particles in boxes.

a) Which diagram could show:

   i) the solution higher in concentration?

   ....

   ii) the mixture of gases at a lower pressure?

   ....

b) If you increase the pressure of a reaction between two gases, does the rate of the reaction **increase** or **decrease**?

....

c) Explain your answer to part **b)**.

....

Q4 Here are four statements about **surface area** and rates of reaction. Circle the correct word or phrase from each pair.

a) Breaking a solid into smaller pieces **increases** / **decreases** its surface area.

b) A larger surface area will mean a **slower** / **faster** rate of reaction.

c) A **larger** / **smaller** surface area decreases the number of collisions.

d) Powdered marble has a **larger** / **smaller** surface area than the same mass of marble chips.

Module C3 — Chemical Economics

Collision Theory

Q5 Choose words from the list below to complete the paragraph.

> speeding up   faster   energy   increases

When a reacting mixture is heated, the particles move ....

This .... how often they collide. It also gives the particles

more .... All this leads to the reaction ....

Q6 Tick the correct box to show whether the statements about catalysts below are **true** or **false**.

		True	False
a)	Catalysts are used up during a reaction.	☐	☐
b)	Only a small amount of catalyst is needed to affect the rate of a reaction.	☐	☐
c)	A catalyst will only work for a particular reaction.	☐	☐

Q7 Circle the correct words to complete the sentences below.

a) In order for a reaction to occur, the particles must **remain still / collide**.

b) If you make a solution more concentrated it means there are **more / less** reactant particles in the same volume.

c) This means that the reactant particles are **more / less** likely to collide with each other.

d) So, increasing the concentration **increases / decreases** the rate of reaction.

Q8 The sign on the right is on the doors of a factory that makes **custard powder**.

> **DANGER**
> NO SMOKING, MATCHES OR OPEN LIGHTS

a) Circle the **two** statements below that are **true**.

- custard powder has a large surface area
- custard powder doesn't burn easily
- custard powder will easily explode
- custard powder has a small surface area

b) Explain why these rules on the sign are important.

....

....

Top Tips: Collision theory is all about reactants bumping into each other. Anything that makes reactants bump into each other more often will increase the rate of the reaction.

Module C3 — Chemical Economics

Rate of Reaction Data

Q1 Sam reacted marble chips with hydrochloric acid. He used two **different concentrations** of acid. He kept everything else the same. The graph below shows the change in the mass of the reactants.

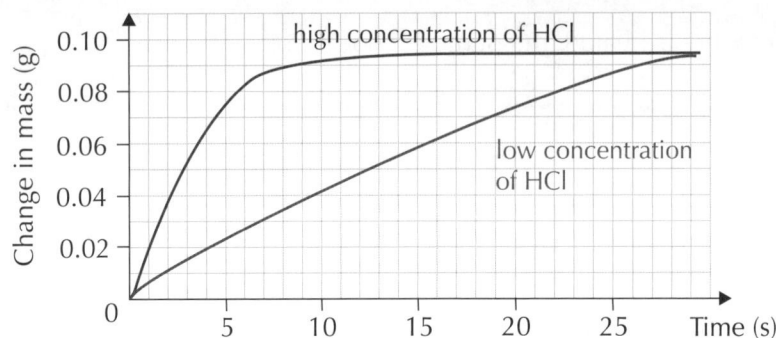

a) Circle the letter(s) next to any valid conclusion(s) below that you might draw **from this graph**.

    A   Increasing the concentration of the acid has no effect on the rate of reaction.

    B   Rate of reaction depends on the acid concentration.

    C   Rate of reaction depends on the mass of the marble chips.

b) The table on the right shows how long it took for the mass to change by 0.02 g in each experiment.

Use the table to state which reaction was **fastest**. Give a reason for your answer.

	Time
High concentration	1 sec
Low concentration	4 sec

....

....

Q2 Eve investigated how **surface area** affects reaction rate. She added excess hydrochloric acid to **large marble chips** and measured the loss of mass at regular times. She repeated the experiment using the same mass of **powdered marble**. Below is a graph of her results.

a) Which curve, A or B, was obtained when **large pieces** of marble were used?

....

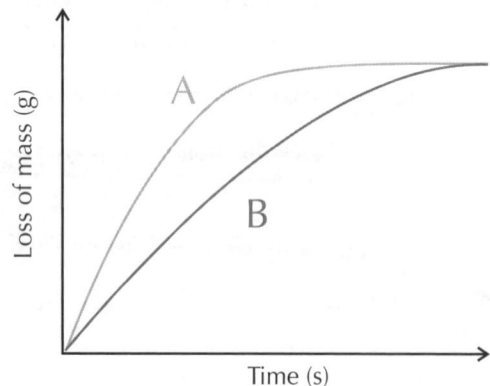

b) On the graph opposite, draw:

    i) the curve you would expect from the **same mass** of **medium-sized** marble pieces. Label it C.

    ii) the curve you would expect from **half the mass** of medium-sized marble pieces. Label it D.

c) Is there enough information given above for you to be sure whether this was a **fair test** or not? Tick the box next to the correct answer.

Yes, because the same mass of marble was used each time. ☐

No, because it is not known if the same concentration of acid was used each time or if the temperature was kept the same. ☐

Module C3 — Chemical Economics

Rate of Reaction Data

Q3 Pete measured how much **carbon dioxide** was given off during the reaction between 5 g of **marble chips** and 100 cm³ of **hydrochloric acid**. His data is shown below.

Time (s)	REACTION 1 Volume of CO_2 produced (cm³)	REACTION 2 Volume of CO_2 produced (cm³)
10	14	24
20	25	42
30	36	57
40	46	69
50	54	77
60	62	80
70	70	80
80	76	80
90	80	80
100	80	80

a) Use the grid below to plot a graph of the data for **reaction 1**. Label it.

b) On the same axes, plot a similar graph for **reaction 2**. Label it.

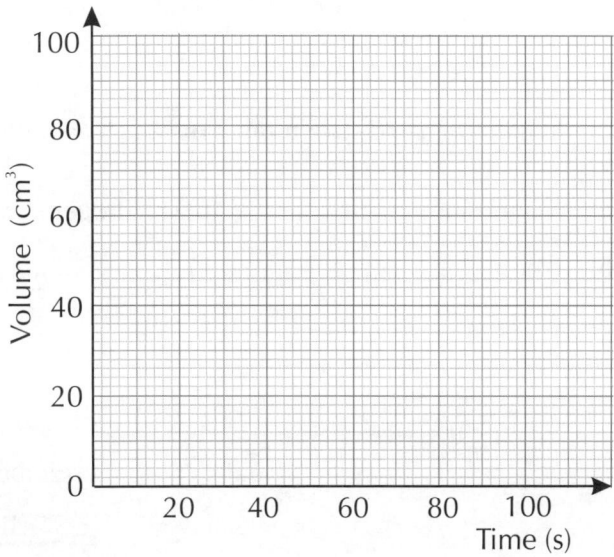

c) On your graph label where reaction 2 had its **fastest rate**.

d) On your graph label where: i) reaction 1 **finished**.
 ii) reaction 2 **finished**.

e) What volume of carbon dioxide had been produced after **25 seconds** in:

   i) reaction 1? ....

   ii) reaction 2? ....

   Read the values off the graph you have drawn.

f) State which reaction is faster. Explain how you know this.

....

g) The difference in the two reaction rates may have been caused by using smaller marble chips which have a larger surface area.

Suggest **two** other possible causes of the difference in **rate** between reaction 1 and reaction 2.

....

....

Top Tips: So, that's it in a nutshell — the faster a reaction goes, the steeper its graph will be, and when the reaction stops, the graph levels out. It's as easy as falling off a chemistry-based log... Ouch...

Module C3 — Chemical Economics

Reacting Masses

Q1 The **relative atomic mass** of an element can be found on the periodic table.

The element helium is shown below as it is on the periodic table. Circle its relative atomic mass.

$${}^{4}_{2}\text{He}$$

Use a periodic table to help you. There's one at the front of this book.

Q2 What are the **relative atomic masses** (A_r) of the following:

a) Magnesium ....   d) Hydrogen ....   g) K ....

b) Neon ....   e) C ....   h) Ca ....

c) Oxygen ....   f) Cu ....   i) Cl ....

Q3 Identify the elements A, B and C.

Element A has an A_r of 4.
Element B has an A_r 3 times that of element A.
Element C has an A_r 4 times that of element A.

Element A = ...

Element B = ...

Element C = ...

Q4 a) Explain how the **relative formula mass** of a **compound** is calculated.

....

b) Calculate the **relative formula masses** (M_r) of:

i) Water, H_2O ....

ii) Potassium hydroxide, KOH ....

iii) Nitric acid, HNO_3 ....

iv) Ammonium nitrate, NH_4NO_3 ....

v) Calcium nitrate, $Ca(NO_3)_2$ ....

vi) Iron(III) hydroxide, $Fe(OH)_3$ ....

Module C3 — Chemical Economics

Reacting Masses

Q5 The **symbol equation** below shows the reaction between calcium and oxygen.

$$2Ca + O_2 \rightarrow 2CaO$$

a) How many atoms of calcium were there at the start of the reaction? ....

b) How many atoms of oxygen were there at the start of the reaction? ....

Q6 The balanced symbol equation below shows a reaction between **propene** and **hydrogen**.

$$C_3H_6 + H_2 \rightarrow C_3H_8$$

a) The **total** relative formula mass of all the reactants is 44.
What is the relative formula mass of the product?

....

b) Circle the correct words in these statements about the reaction above.

   i) The total mass of reactants is **the same as / different to** the mass of the product.

   ii) This is because the number of atoms at the start of a reaction is
   the same as / different to the number at the end.

   iii) This is called 'the principle of **conservation / variation** of mass'.

Q7 18 g of **calcium oxide** were reacted with some **water**. **Calcium hydroxide** was formed.

a) Write down the word equation for this reaction.

....

b) Circle the correct words in the sentences below.

Atoms **are / aren't** made or lost during a reaction.

So, the mass of the reactants is **the same as / different from** the mass of the products.

c) The mass of the product, calcium hydroxide, at the end of the reaction was 29 g.
What mass of water was used?

....

....

Module C3 — Chemical Economics

Calculating Masses in Reactions

Q1 **Sodium** burns in air to produce **sodium oxide**.
The limiting reactant in this reaction is sodium.

Tick the correct box below to show which statement is true.

☐ If the amount of sodium is **doubled** then the amount of sodium oxide produced will **halve**.

☐ If the amount of sodium is **halved** then the amount of sodium oxide produced will **double**.

☐ If the amount of sodium is **doubled** then the amount of sodium oxide produced will **double**.

Q2 **Propane** burns in **oxygen** to give **carbon dioxide** and **water**.

The table below shows the masses of the reactants and the products in three different experiments of this reaction. Complete the table below by filling in the missing masses.

Mass of compound (g)			
propane	oxygen	carbon dioxide	water
22	80	66	36
11		33	18
44	160	132	

Q3 **Calcium** reacts with **oxygen** to produce **calcium oxide**.

a) Balance the **symbol equation** for this reaction.

You won't need to write numbers on all of the lines.

$$\ldots\ldots Ca + \ldots\ldots O_2 \rightarrow \ldots\ldots CaO$$

b) **40 g** of calcium burns in air to give **56 g** of calcium oxide.
What mass of oxygen reacted?

....

c) **2 g** of calcium reacts with **0.8 g** of oxygen.
What mass of calcium oxide is produced?

....

d) **22.4 g** of calcium oxide is produced when calcium is burnt in **6.4 g** of oxygen.
What mass of calcium reacted?

....

Module C3 — Chemical Economics

Calculating Masses in Reactions

Q4 When heated, **limestone** ($CaCO_3$) decomposes (breaks down). **Calcium oxide** (CaO) and **carbon dioxide** (CO_2) are made.

a) Write a balanced symbol equation for this reaction.

....

b) **100 g** of limestone decomposes to form **44 g** of carbon dioxide. What mass of calcium oxide is produced?

....

c) Calculate the mass of limestone that decomposes to produce **14 g** of calcium oxide and **11 g** of carbon dioxide.

....

Q5 Anna reacts **magnesium** (Mg) with **oxygen** (O_2) to produce **magnesium oxide** (MgO).

a) Write a **balanced symbol equation** for this reaction.

....

To balance the equation make sure the number of each type of atom is the same on both sides.

b) **12 g** of magnesium reacts with **8 g** of oxygen in the reaction. Calculate the mass of **magnesium oxide** produced.

....

....

c) **10 g** of magnesium is burnt and **16.7 g** of magnesium oxide is produced. Calculate the mass of **oxygen** used in the reaction.

....

....

Q6 **Aluminium** and **iron oxide** (Fe_2O_3) react together to produce **aluminium oxide** (Al_2O_3) and **iron**.

a) Balance the **symbol equation** for this reaction.

You won't need to write numbers on all of the lines.

$$\ldots\ldots Al + \ldots\ldots Fe_2O_3 \rightarrow \ldots\ldots Al_2O_3 + \ldots\ldots Fe$$

b) **13.5 g** of aluminium reacts with **40 g** of iron oxide. How much aluminium reacts with **80 g** iron oxide?

....

....

Module C3 — Chemical Economics

Atom Economy

Q1 In the chemical industry it is important that reactions have a high atom economy. Circle the correct words in the following paragraph.

> The atom economy of a reaction tells you the amount of atoms that are **wasted** / **created** when making a chemical. **0%** / **100%** atom economy means that all the atoms in the reactants have been turned into useful products. The **higher** / **lower** the atom economy the 'greener' the process.

Q2 The atom economy of a reaction can be **calculated** using a **formula**.

Use the words below to complete the formula.

M_r of desired products   Sum of M_r of all products

$$\text{Atom economy} = \frac{\ldots\ldots\ldots\ldots\ldots\ldots\ldots\ldots\ldots\ldots}{\ldots\ldots\ldots\ldots\ldots\ldots\ldots\ldots\ldots\ldots} \times 100$$

Q3 **Potassium hydroxide** can be reacted with hydrochloric acid to produce potassium chloride.

> potassium hydroxide + hydrochloric acid → potassium chloride + water
> $KOH + HCl \rightarrow KCl + H_2O$
> Relative formula masses: **KOH = 56, HCl = 36.5, KCl = 74.5, H_2O = 18**

a) What is the desired product in this reaction? ....

b) Calculate the **atom economy** of the reaction. ....

....

Q4 The two reactions shown below are both used industrially to make **ethanol** (CH_3CH_2OH).

Reaction 1: $C_2H_4 + H_2O \rightarrow CH_3CH_2OH$ Reaction 2: $C_6H_{12}O_6 \rightarrow 2CH_3CH_2OH + 2CO_2$

a) State which of these two reactions has a 100% atom economy. ....

b) Give a reason for your answer to part **a)**.

....

....

Module C3 — Chemical Economics

Percentage Yield

Q1 Complete the following sentences:

a) A 100% yield means ....

b) A 0% yield means ....

Q2 Match each of the following to the reason why it would affect the percentage yield of a reaction.

Filtration — Some of the liquid remains in the old container.

Evaporation — You lose some of the liquid or solid.

Heating — This can change the amount of product that's formed.

Transferring liquids — This happens all the time, not just whilst heating, causing some liquid to be lost.

Q3 Tick the correct box to say whether the following statements are true or false.

		True	False
a)	The predicted yield is how much product you expect to get from the reaction.	☐	☐
b)	The percentage yield is how much product you got from doing the reaction compared to how much product you expected to get.	☐	☐
c)	You can get a percentage yield of more than 100%.	☐	☐
d)	All the reactants always react to make a product.	☐	☐
e)	In an experiment you can get a percentage yield of 100%.	☐	☐
f)	The actual yield is how much product you end up with.	☐	☐

Q4 The percentage yield of a reaction can be calculated using a formula.

Use the words below to complete the formula.

actual yield   predicted yield

Oh joy, another page with maths on it.

$$\text{Percentage yield} = \frac{\text{..}}{\text{..}} \times 100$$

Module C3 — Chemical Economics

Percentage Yield

Q5 Aaliya and Natasha made some **barium sulfate** using barium chloride and sodium sulfate. They used the following method:

1. Using a measuring cylinder, measure out 25 cm³ of barium chloride solution. Add the barium chloride solution to a beaker containing sodium sulfate solution.

2. An insoluble precipitate will form in the beaker. Filter the contents of the beaker through filter paper.

3. Rinse the solid with distilled water and put it on to a clean piece of filter paper to dry.

Aaliya calculated that they should produce a yield of **15 g** of barium sulfate. However, after completing the experiment they found they had only obtained **6 g**.

a) Suggest how material was lost at each step in the method:

Step 1. ....

Step 2. ....

Step 3. ....

b) Calculate the percentage yield for this reaction.

....

Q6 Calculate the **percentage yield** for the following reactions.

a) Reaction 1: actual yield = 15.4 g, predicted yield = 22 g

....

....

b) Reaction 2: actual yield = 4.6 g, predicted yield = 13.8 g

....

....

c) Reaction 3: actual yield = 16 g, predicted yield = 20 g

....

....

d) Reaction 4: actual yield = 1.3 g, predicted yield = 2.8 g

....

....

Module C3 — Chemical Economics

Chemical Production

Q1 Connect the **types** of chemical production with the statements that **describe them**.

- Batch production — Chemicals are only made when they are needed.
- Continuous production — Chemicals are made all the time.

Q2 Lots of things affect how much it **costs** to research and make a drug.

Draw a line between each factor that affects the cost of making a drug and its explanation. One has been done for you.

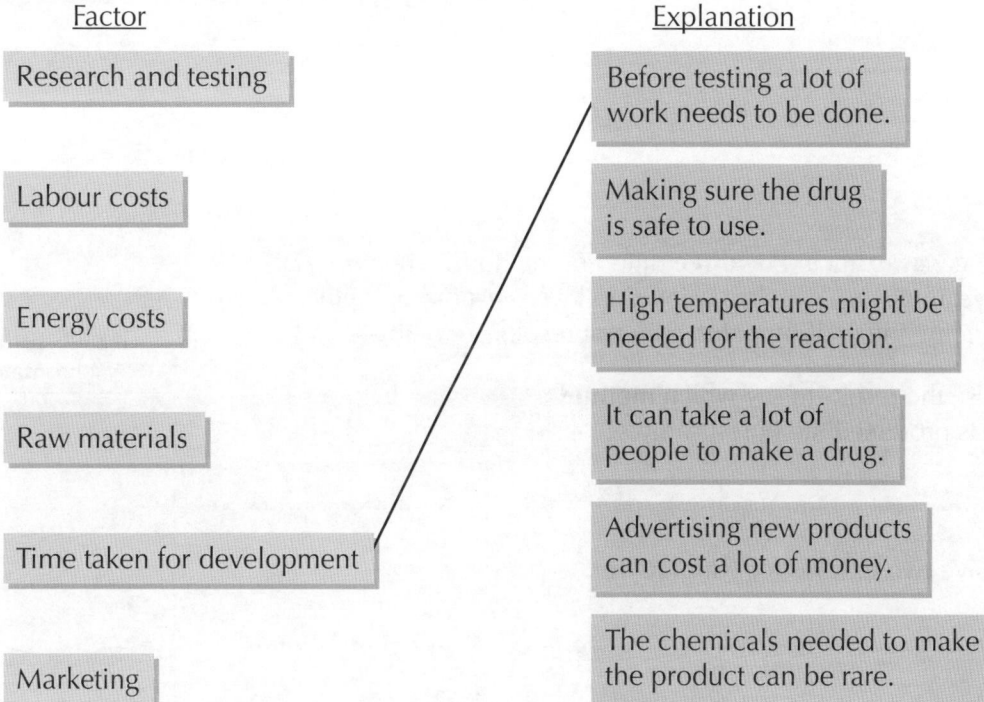

Factor	Explanation
Research and testing	Before testing a lot of work needs to be done.
Labour costs	Making sure the drug is safe to use.
Energy costs	High temperatures might be needed for the reaction.
Raw materials	It can take a lot of people to make a drug.
Time taken for development	Advertising new products can cost a lot of money.
Marketing	The chemicals needed to make the product can be rare.

Q3 Different chemicals are made using different **production methods**.

a) i) Circle the type of production method that is used to make **ammonia**.

   batch production   **continuous production**

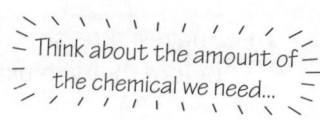

Think about the amount of the chemical we need...

   ii) Give a reason for your answer.

   ....

b) i) Circle the type of production method that is used to make **pharmaceuticals** (drugs).

   batch production   **continuous production**

   ii) Give a reason for your answer.

   ....

Chemical Production

Q4 Tony decides his pharmaceutical company should develop and make a new **drug**.

Compounds used in pharmaceutical drugs are often extracted from **plants**.
Below are three steps in the extraction of a chemical from a plant.

 **Step A:** Dissolve the substance in a suitable solvent.

 **Step B:** Crush the plant.

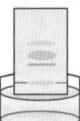 **Step C:** Extract the substance using chromatography.

a) Put the steps A, B and C in the correct order.   1. Step ....   2. Step ....   3. Step ....

b) Compounds that are used to make drugs can also be made in the lab.
Circle the correct word that describes these compounds.

    energetic   synthetic   chromatographic   purple

Q5 A drug was extracted by **three** different methods. The purity of each sample was checked using **thin layer chromatography** and by finding the **melting point**. The test results are below.

Results using thin layer chromatography.

a) i) Use the results to say **which method** has produced the purest sample.

....

ii) Give **two** reasons for your answer.

....

....

....

| | Method 1 | Method 2 | Method 3 |

b) Suggest a reason why it is important to check that drugs are pure before they are used.

....

....

....

	Melting temperature (°C)
Pure sample	82
Method 1	80
Method 2	82
Method 3	76

Module C3 — Chemical Economics

Allotropes of Carbon

Q1 Diamond, graphite, and fullerenes are all allotropes of carbon.

a) What is an **allotrope**? Circle the answer.

An allotrope is a different structural form of the same element in the same physical state.

An allotrope is a hollow ball or tube-like structure.

An allotrope is a substance that can conduct electricity.

b) The structures of **three** allotropes of carbon are shown below. Label each allotrope using the names below.

diamond   Buckminster fullerene   graphite

i)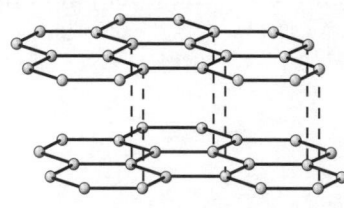

ii)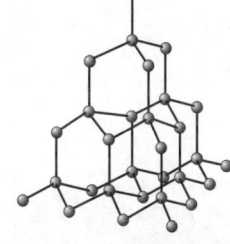

....

iii)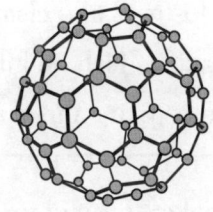

....

Q2 Nanotubes and fullerenes are types of nanoparticles.

a) Give **two** uses of nanotubes.

....

....

b) Explain why fullerenes can be used to deliver drugs.

....

....

Top Tips: There's more than one allotrope of carbon you've got to know about and you need to know what they are, what their uses are and why they're suitable for these uses. Hmmm, thrilling.

Module C3 — Chemical Economics

Allotropes of Carbon

Q3 **Graphite** is an allotrope of carbon.

a) Fill in the gaps in the passage using words from the list below.

> slippery   opaque   lustrous
>
> Graphite is black and .... (you can't see through it).
>
> It is also .... (shiny). The layers in graphite slide over each easily
>
> which makes it .... and useful as a lubricant.

b) Describe why graphite is useful for making pencil leads.

....

Q4 **Diamond** is another allotrope of carbon.

a) Circle the correct words to complete the sentences below about diamond.

> Diamond is **black / colourless**, lustrous and **clear / opaque**. It has lots of
> strong bonds so diamond has a **low / high** melting point and is very **soft / hard**.
> Diamond **can / can't** conduct electricity and **is / isn't** soluble in water.

b) Name a property of diamond that makes it useful for **jewellery**.

....

c) Name a property of diamond that makes it useful for **cutting tools**.

....

Q5 The sentences below each contain **one** mistake. Write out the correct versions of the sentences.

a) Graphite and diamond both form small molecular structures.

....

b) This is because carbon cannot form many bonds with itself.

....

Module C3 — Chemical Economics

Mixed Questions — Module C3

Q1 Lee is investigating how the **concentration** of acid affects the rate of a reaction.

a) The diagram on the right shows the acid particles present in a solution of **dilute acid**.

In the box, complete the diagram showing the **same volume** of **concentrated acid**.

b) Circle the sentence that describes what would happen to the rate of reaction if the **concentration** of the acid was **increased**.

| Increasing the concentration of acid would decrease the rate of reaction. | Increasing the concentration of acid would not affect the rate of reaction. | Increasing the concentration of acid would increase the rate of reaction. |

c) The graph on the right shows the results of two **rate of reaction experiments** using dilute and concentrated acid.

   i) Which line shows the reaction using dilute acid, P or Q?

   ....

   ii) Give a reason for your answer.

   ....

   ....

Q2 A sample of fuel X was burnt and used to heat **100 g** of water. The temperature of the water before heating was **20 °C**, and after heating it was **42 °C**.

a) Calculate the change in temperature of the water during the experiment.

....

b) The formula for calculating the energy transferred in a reaction is:

Energy transferred (J) = mass of water (g) × 4.2 × change in temperature (°C)

Calculate the energy transferred in this reaction.

....

....

....

c) Circle the name is given to a reaction like this one that gives out energy to its surroundings.

    endothermic   exothermic   neutralisation

Module C3 — Chemical Economics

Mixed Questions — Module C3

Q3 Many important medicines are made using **plants**. Give the **three** steps that are needed to extract a useful chemical from plant material.

1. ....

2. ....

3. ....

Q4 The **Haber Process** is used to manufacture **ammonia** (NH_3). The reactants are **hydrogen gas** (H_2) and **nitrogen gas** (N_2).

a) Calculate the **relative formula mass** of ammonia.
   (A_r of N = 14, A_r of H = 1)

   ....

b) Write a **word equation** for the reaction that creates ammonia.

   ....

c) Write a **balanced symbol equation** for the same reaction.

   ....

d) If **14 g** of nitrogen completely reacts with **3 g** of hydrogen it produces **17 g** of ammonia. How much nitrogen will be needed to produce **34 g** of ammonia if it completely reacts?

   ....

   ....

e) The predicted yield for an experiment was **18 g** of ammonia but the actual yield was about **2.25 g**. Calculate the percentage yield of the reaction.

   ....

   ....

f) A solid iron catalyst is added to the reaction mixture. Circle the correct words to complete the following sentences about the catalyst.

   i) Adding a catalyst can **increase / decrease** the rate of a reaction.

   ii) The catalyst **is / isn't** used up during the reaction.

g) Ammonia is usually produced using **continuous production** not **batch** production. Give one **difference** between continuous and batch production.

   ....

Module C3 — Chemical Economics

Module P3 — Forces for Transport

Speed and Velocity

Q1 I rode my bike **1500 m** to the shops. It took me **300 seconds**.

average speed = distance ÷ time

a) What was my **average speed** in m/s?

....

b) I took a different route home that was **1920 m**. It took me **480 s**. What was my **average speed** in m/s?

....

c) Use this equation to answer the following questions:

$$\text{distance} = \frac{(u + v)}{2} \times t$$

Remember, u is the speed at the start and v is the speed at the end.

i) One part of the journey was downhill. I was travelling at **4 m/s** at the top of the hill and **11 m/s** at the bottom. It took **48 s** to get from the top of the hill to the bottom. What **distance** did I cover on this part of the journey?

....

....

ii) I was travelling at **6 m/s** when I hit the brakes. It took **3 s** to stop. What **distance** did I travel while braking?

....

....

Q2 Ealing is about **12 km** west of Marble Arch. It takes a tube train **20 minutes** to get to Marble Arch from Ealing.

Circle the letter next to the true statement below.

A The average speed of the train is 60 m/s.
B The average speed of the train is 10 m/s.
C The average speed of the train is 60 m/s due east.
D The average speed of the train is 36 m/s.

Q3 The monorail at a theme park takes people from the visitor centre to the main park and back again. It travels at the **same speed** on the outward and return journeys.

The monorail's **velocity** on the outward journey is **+12 m/s**. What is its velocity on the return journey?

....

Speed and Distance

Q1 The distance-time graph shows the movement of a **train**. It travels from Alphaville to Charlietown, where it **stops** briefly, and then moves off again.

a) Describe the **movement** of the train in the sections marked:

A ....

B ....

C ....

D ....

b) How long does the train **stop** at Charlietown?

....

c) i) How long does it take the train to travel between Alphaville and Charlietown?

....

ii) What is the distance between Alphaville and Charlietown?

....

iii) What is the train's **average speed** between Alphaville and Charlietown?

....

Use your answers to parts i) and ii) to work this out.

....

Q2 Dan gets caught speeding by a **speed camera**.

a) Number the statements (1-5) to explain how speed cameras can measure the speed of a car whizzing by. The first one is done for you.

- [1] White lines are painted on the road at equal distances apart.
- [ ] The photos show the distance travelled by the car in the time between the photos.
- [ ] The car's speed is calculated from the distance travelled and the time between the photos.
- [ ] A second photo is taken a short time later.
- [ ] A photo of the car is taken as it passes the first line.

b) Two photos are taken **0.5 seconds** apart. In that time Dan travels **7 m**. How fast was Dan going? Give your answer in m/s.

....

....

Module P3 — Forces for Transport

Speed and Acceleration

Q1 An egg is **dropped** from the top of the Eiffel tower. It hits the ground after **8 seconds**, at a speed of **80 m/s**.

Use the following equation to find the egg's acceleration.

$$\text{acceleration} = \frac{\text{change in speed}}{\text{time taken}}$$

....

....

Q2 a) A car **accelerates** from rest to **20 m/s** in **2.5 s**. What is its **acceleration**?

....

....

b) A second car **decelerates** from **20 m/s** to **4 m/s** in **4 s**. What is its **deceleration**?

....

....

Q3 The **speed-time graph** on the right shows a speed-skater's performance during a race.

a) Describe the motion of the skater in the following sections:

X ....

....

Y ....

....

Z ....

....

b) Work out the **distance** travelled in **section Z**.

....

....

Module P3 — Forces for Transport

Speed and Acceleration

Q4 Use the information in the table to draw a **speed-time** graph on the axes below.

Time (s)	Speed (m/s)
0	0
5	4
10	8
15	12
20	12
25	9
30	6
35	3
40	0
45	0

Q5 Jimmy is playing with his radio-controlled car in the park and decides to plot a speed-time graph for the car.

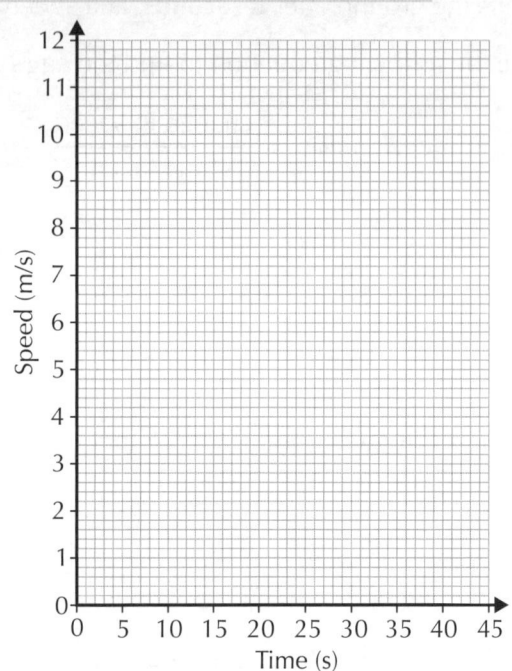

a) What does the area under the graph tell you?

....

....

b) Work out the distance travelled by the car:

i) between 5 and 15 seconds.

....

ii) between 20 and 30 seconds.

....

c) The graph shows that the car accelerated from **rest** to **4.5 m/s** in **5 seconds**. Calculate the acceleration of the car.

....

....

Top Tips: The most confusing thing about acceleration can be the graphs. Remember that on a speed-time graph the steepness of the line is the Acceleration. The steeper the line, the greater the acceleration. Make sure you know what the area under the graph means too. Learn these facts and the graphs won't just look like a bunch of lines — they'll look like lines... but with meaning.

Module P3 — Forces for Transport

Forces

Q1 Circle any of the situations below where the forces are **balanced**.

An accelerating car

A cow falling at its terminal speed

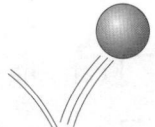
A ball bouncing upwards

A book sat on a table

Q2 A **teapot** sits on a table.

a) Explain why it **doesn't** sink into the table.

....

b) Jane picks up the teapot and hangs it from the ceiling by a rope. What **vertical** forces now act on the teapot?

....

....

c) The rope breaks and the teapot accelerates towards the floor. Are the vertical forces **balanced**? Circle the answer.

Yes   No

Q3 A bear weighing **700 N** rides a bike at a **constant speed** with a driving force of **1500 N**.

Label the forces shown on the diagram. Include the size of each force.

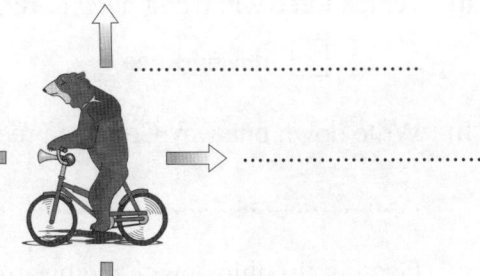

Module P3 — Forces for Transport

Friction

Q1 Circle the letter next to the correct answer to complete the following sentence.

The Moon does not feel a drag force because...

    A ... there is no atmosphere in space.

    B ... it is orbiting the Earth

    C ... there is no gravity in space.

Q2 Tick the box next to the change which will **not** reduce the drag force on an aeroplane.

- ☐ flying higher (where there is less air)
- ☐ flying more slowly
- ☐ carrying fewer bags and people
- ☐ making the plane more streamlined

Q3 On the way down a slide, a penguin experiences **friction**.

  a) Between which two surfaces is friction acting?

....

  b) On the picture, draw an arrow to show the **direction** in which friction is acting on the penguin.

  c) Suggest how the penguin could speed up his slide. Circle all correct answers.

    By kicking his flippers and feet up and down.   **By putting a layer of grease on the slide.**   **By making himself more streamlined.**

Q4 Geoff is trying to design the ultimate caravan with the highest top speed possible.

  a) Which force will Geoff need to **reduce** if he wants his caravan to go faster? Tick **one** box.

    ☐ driving force   ☐ gravity   ☐ air resistance

  b) Write down **one** way Geoff can reduce this force on the caravan.

....

  c) Geoff is also thinking of adding a roof box on top of the caravan. Would this increase or decrease its top speed? Circle the correct answer. **increase / decrease**

Module P3 — Forces for Transport

Weight and Terminal Speed

Q1 Tick the boxes to show whether the following statements are **true** or **false**.

		True	False
a)	Any object falling to Earth will have the same acceleration due to gravity.	☐	☐
b)	An object will have a different mass on the Moon than on the Earth.	☐	☐
c)	Weight is caused by a gravitational field acting on a mass.	☐	☐

Q2 Complete the passage about a **sky-diver** using the words from the box.

greater   equals   terminal   accelerates   zero   increase
When a sky-diver jumps out of a plane, the force of gravity pulling him down is .... than the frictional force slowing him down, so he .... downwards. This causes the frictional force to .... until it .... the force of gravity. At this point, the overall force is .... — the sky-diver is at .... speed.

Q3 Daisy visits three different planets which have different gravitational field strengths. Daisy has a mass of **300 kg**. Calculate her **weight** on each planet.

weight = mass × gravitational field strength

Planet: Krikkit
Gravitational field strength: 9.2 m/s²
....
....
....

Planet: Zenn-La
Gravitational field strength: 3.8 m/s²
....
....
....

Planet: Gallifrey
Gravitational field strength: 1.3 m/s²
....
....
....

Module P3 — Forces for Transport

Forces and Acceleration

Q1 Complete the passage below using the words from the box.

> smaller   bigger   accelerate   constant   balanced

If the forces on an object are all .... , then it will move at a .... speed in the same direction. If not, the object will .... in the direction of the force. The .... the force you push with, the greater the acceleration. The bigger the mass of the object, the .... the acceleration for the same force.

Q2 You're travelling home from school on a bus doing a **steady speed** in a **straight line**. Tick the boxes next to all the statements that are **true**.

☐ The driving force of the engine is bigger than friction and air resistance combined.
☐ There are no forces acting on the bus.
☐ The driving force of the engine is equal to friction and air resistance combined.
☐ No force is required to keep the bus moving.

Q3 Circle the correct words to complete the sentences below.

> If there is **a balanced** / **an unbalanced** force acting on an object, it will accelerate in the **opposite** / **same** direction to/as the force. The size of the acceleration can be calculated using $F = m \times a$ / $F = m \div a$.

Q4 Work out the resultant force on each car to complete the table.

Car	Mass (kg)	Acceleration (m/s²)	Resultant Force (N)
Disraeli 9000	800	5	
Palmerston 6i	1560	0.7	
Heath TT	950	3	
Asquith 380	790	2	

Module P3 — Forces for Transport

Forces and Acceleration

Q5 Jo and Brian have fitted both their scooters with the **same engine**. Brian and his scooter have a combined mass of **110 kg** and a maximum acceleration of **2.80 m/s²**. On her scooter, Jo only manages an acceleration of **1.71 m/s²**.

a) What **force** can the engine exert at Brian's maximum acceleration?

....

....

b) Calculate the combined **mass** of Jo and her scooter.

You'll need to rearrange the force, mass and acceleration formula. The force will be the same as part a).

....

....

Q6 State whether or not the forces acting on the following objects are **balanced**, and explain your reasoning.

a) A cricket ball rolling at a constant speed along the ground.

....

....

b) A car slowing down at the end of a journey.

....

....

c) A vase falling to the floor.

....

....

d) A space rocket slowing down as it enters the Earth's atmosphere.

....

....

e) A bag of rubbish travelling at a constant speed through deep space.

....

....

Top Tips: A resultant force means your object will accelerate — it will change its speed or direction (or both). But if your object has a constant speed (which could be zero) and a constant direction, you can say with utter confidence that there ain't any resultant force. Be careful though — a zero resultant force doesn't mean there are **no** forces, just that they all balance each other out.

Module P3 — Forces for Transport

Stopping Distances

Q1 The distance a car takes to stop is split up into **thinking** distance and **braking** distance.

a) What is meant by the 'braking distance'? Circle the correct answer.

| The distance taken to stop once the brakes have been applied. | The distance you travel before you apply the brakes. |

b) What is meant by the 'thinking distance'? Tick the box next to the correct answer.

☐ The distance you think the car will travel when you've applied the brakes.

☐ The distance the car travels in the time between the need for braking occurring and the brakes starting to act.

c) Explain why a **tired** driver has a greater thinking distance.

....

....

Q2 Tick the boxes to show whether the following statements are **true** or **false**.

		True	False
a)	Tyres have a tread so they grip onto the water in wet weather.	☐	☐
b)	The braking distance will be the same for all road surfaces.	☐	☐
c)	The more heavily a car is loaded, the shorter its stopping distance.	☐	☐
d)	The total stopping distance is the thinking distance + the braking distance.	☐	☐

Q3 Will the following factors affect **thinking** distance, **braking** distance or **both**? Write the words below in the correct columns in the table.

tiredness   alcohol   ice   speed   tyres   road surface   brakes   load

Thinking Distance	Braking Distance	Both

Module P3 — Forces for Transport

More on Stopping Distances

Q1 Use the information given below on typical stopping distances to answer the questions.

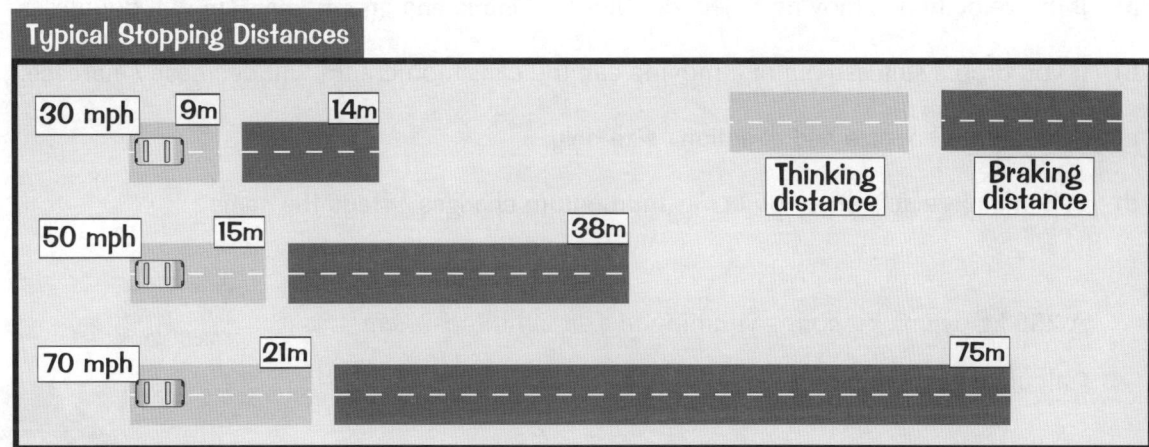

a) What is the **thinking distance** of a car travelling at **50 mph**? Circle the answer.

      15 m   38 m   9 m

b) What is the **braking distance** of a car travelling at **70 mph**? Circle the answer.

      21 m   75 m   14 m

c) Calculate the total stopping distance for a car travelling at **30 mph**.

....

....

Q2 Circle the correct word in each pair to complete the sentences below.

> To avoid an accident, drivers need to leave a **large / small** gap between their car and the one in front. This is so that if they had to **accelerate quickly / stop suddenly** they would have time to do it safely. Speed limits are really important because your speed affects the **accelerating / stopping** distance so much. Even at 30 mph, you should drive no closer than **1 or 2 / 6 or 7** car lengths away from the car in front — just in case.

Top Tips: All this stuff on stopping distance gives me the heebie jeebies. It'll take you a whopping 96 m (about the length of a football pitch) to stop if you're travelling at 70 mph. If you're travelling too close to the car in front you've got no chance of stopping in time — you have been warned.

Module P3 — Forces for Transport

Momentum

Q1 Circle the correct words to complete the following sentences.

a) If the velocity of a moving object doubles, its **kinetic energy** / **momentum** will double.

b) If you drop a suitcase out of a moving car, the car's momentum will **decrease** / **increase**.

c) Momentum has **size and direction** / **size only**.

d) When a force acts on an object its momentum **changes** / **stays the same**.

Q2 A **250 kg** pygmy hippo is swimming in a straight line at **3 m/s**. Calculate its momentum.

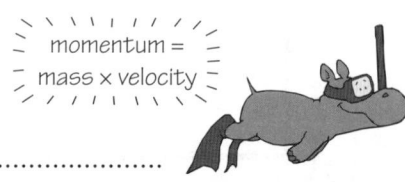
momentum = mass × velocity

....

....

Q3 Circle the correct word in each pair to complete the passage below.

> If the time taken for an object to change momentum is small, the force acting will be **small** / **large**. So if someone's momentum changes very quickly (like in a collision), the forces on the body will be very **large** / **small**, and **more** / **less** likely to cause injury.

Q4 Place the following four trucks in order of increasing momentum.

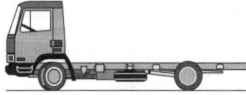  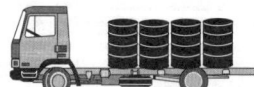 

Truck A	Truck B	Truck C	Truck D
velocity = 30 m/s	velocity = 10 m/s	velocity = 20 m/s	velocity = 15 m/s
mass = 3000 kg	mass = 4500 kg	mass = 4000 kg	mass = 3500 kg

....

....

....

....

(lowest momentum)   .... , ... , ... , ...   (highest momentum)

Momentum

Q5 Jemima has a mass of **30 kg** and is waddling in a straight line away from a walrus. Her momentum is **36 kg m/s**. Calculate Jemima's velocity.

You'll need to rearrange the momentum formula.

....

....

....

Q6 A boat was travelling through the water in a straight line at constant speed. A wave hit the side of the boat. The collision caused a change in momentum of **9600 kg m/s** and lasted for **1.2 seconds**.

a) Calculate the force acting on the boat as the wave hits it.

force = change in momentum ÷ time

....

....

b) A few minutes later, the boat was hit by another wave. The boat's **change** in momentum was **the same** as last time, but the force of the wave acted over a **shorter time**.

What was the size of the force acting on the boat during the second wave? Circle the answer.

    Larger than the force of the first wave.   The same as the force of the first wave.   Smaller than the force of the first wave.

Q7 A **1200 kg** car is travelling at **30 m/s** along the motorway. It crashes into the barrier of the central reservation and is stopped in **1.2 seconds**.

a) Find the momentum of the car **before** the crash.

....

....

b) Find the size of the **average force** acting on the car as it stops.

....

....

Top Tips: The main thing to remember about momentum (apart from how to use the equation) is that it **changes** when a resultant force acts on an object. So if a fast car started to brake, there'd be a resultant backwards force, and the car's momentum would decrease. Makes perfect sense really.

Module P3 — Forces for Transport

Car Safety

Q1 Complete this passage by using the words in the box.

| crashing | tested | sensors | dummies | data |

Safety features are .... to see how effectively they save lives or stop injuries in an accident. Test .... is gathered by .... cars containing crash test .... both with and without safety features in place. They have .... at different places on their bodies to show where, and how badly, a real person would be injured.

Q2 a) Circle the correct word in each pair to complete the passage on **seat belts**.

A seat belt is designed so that it **stretches slightly / stays the same shape** during an impact. This **increases / reduces** the forces acting on the passengers and absorbs energy. After a crash, seat belts have to be **replaced / recycled** in case they have been weakened.

b) Name **two other** safety features that absorb energy.

1. .... 2. ....

Q3 A car **brakes** to avoid hitting a **giant statue of a cat**. The car is fitted with a number of features that improve the **safety** of the car.

a) What type of **energy** does the car have because it's **moving**? Circle the answer.

electrical   kinetic   potential   sound

b) The car skids and hits the cat statue. Name **one** safety feature that could have prevented this.

....

c) Why are many car safety features designed to slow down the car and the people inside over the **longest possible time** in a collision?

....

....

d) The car is fitted with a **safety cage**. Explain how this protects the people inside the car.

....

....

Module P3 — Forces for Transport

Work Done and Power

Q1 Circle the correct words to complete the following sentences.

a) Work involves the transfer of **force** / **energy**.

b) To do work a **force** / **push** acts over **a distance** / **time**.

c) Work done is measured in **watts** / **joules**.

Q2 Complete this passage by using the words below.

You won't need to use all of the words.

    watts   rate   joules   kilograms

Power is the .... of doing work, or how quickly work is being done. It is measured in .... or .... of energy transferred per second.

Q3 An elephant uses **1200 N** to push a donkey along a track.

work done = force × distance

Calculate the work done by the elephant if the donkey moves **8 m**.

....

....

Q4 Ben's weight is **600 N**. He climbs a ladder. The rungs of the ladder are **0.2 m** apart.

a) What force is Ben doing work **against** as he climbs?

....

b) How much work does Ben do when he climbs **10 rungs**?

....

....

c) What distance does Ben have to climb before he has done **15 000 J** of work?

You'll need to rearrange the work done formula.

....

....

Module P3 — Forces for Transport

Work Done and Power

Q5 Jenny kicks a football, giving it **5000 J** of energy.

a) How much work does Jenny do?

....

b) If Jenny kicks the ball with a force of **250 N**, over what **distance** does her kick act on the ball?

You'll need to rearrange the work done formula.

....

....

Q6 Catherine and Sally decide to have a race to see who can get to the ice cream van first. Catherine won the race in **6.2 s**, while Sally took **6.4 s**. They both did **1200 J** of work.

Find each girl's power output during the run.

power = work done ÷ time taken

....

....

....

Q7 Josie runs home after school so she can watch her favourite TV programme.

a) She runs a distance of **24 m** and exerts a force of **88 N**. Calculate the work done by Josie on her run.

....

....

b) Her run takes **6 s**. Calculate her power over the run.

....

....

Q8 A sports car transfers **2 650 000 kJ** of chemical energy **per hour** into kinetic energy. Calculate its power.

You need to change the units into joules and seconds.

....

....

....

Module P3 — Forces for Transport

Kinetic and Gravitational Potential Energy

Q1 Tick the boxes to show whether the following statements are **true** or **false**.

		True	False
a)	Gravitational potential energy = mass × g × height.	☐	☐
b)	The kinetic energy of something is the energy it has when it's not moving.	☐	☐
c)	On Earth, the gravitational field strength is approximately 10 N/kg.	☐	☐
d)	If you double the mass of a moving object, the kinetic energy doubles.	☐	☐
e)	On Earth, a 3 kg chicken flies up 2.5 m to sit on a fence. It gains about 75 J of gravitational potential energy.	☐	☐

Q2 Find the kinetic energy of a **200 kg** bear running at a speed of **9 m/s**.

kinetic energy = ½ × mass × speed²

....

....

Q3 Tick the box next to the vehicle which has the **greatest kinetic energy**.

☐ 60 000 kg, 5 m/s   ☐ 100 kg, 8 m/s   ☐ 1200 kg, 20 m/s

....

....

Q4 A car of mass **1000 kg** travels at **10 m/s**.

a) Calculate its kinetic energy.

....

....

b) Tick the boxes next to all the statements below that are **true**.

Kinetic energy is energy due to movement. ☐

If a driver doubles her speed, her kinetic energy will be twice as big. ☐

The kinetic energy of the car just depends of how fast it is travelling. ☐

Module P3 — Forces for Transport

Kinetic and Gravitational Potential Energy

Q5 Mike has bought some dumb-bells to help him get buff. He has one **5 kg** dumb-bell and one **10 kg** dumb-bell stored on the same shelf.

a) Which dumb-bell has more gravitational potential energy? Circle the correct answer.

   5 kg   10 kg   They both have the same gravitational potential energy.

b) Mike moves the 10 kg dumb-bell to a lower shelf. What happens to its gravitational potential energy? Circle the correct answer.

   increases   decreases   stays the same

Q6 A large truck and a car are both travelling at a speed of **22 m/s**. The mass of the truck is **12 288 kg** and the mass of the car is **1200 kg**.

kinetic energy = ½ × mass × speed²

a) Calculate the kinetic energy of:

   i) the car ....

   ii) the truck ....

b) John is playing with his remote-controlled toy car and truck. The car's mass is **100 g**. The truck's mass is **300 g**. The car is moving **twice as fast** as the truck. Which has more kinetic energy? Circle the answer.

   Work out how many times bigger the kinetic energy is when you triple the mass, and when you double the speed.

   car   truck

Q7 Dave works at a DIY shop. He has to load **28 flagstones** onto the delivery truck. Each flagstone has a mass of **25 kg** and has to be lifted **1.2 m** onto the truck.

a) How much gravitational potential energy does **one** flagstone **gain** when lifted onto the truck? (g = 10 m/s²)

   G.P.E. = mass × g × height

   ....

b) What is the **total** gravitational potential energy gained by the flagstones after they are all loaded onto the truck?

   ....

Module P3 — Forces for Transport

Falling Objects and Roller Coasters

Q1 A toy cricket ball hit straight upwards has a gravitational potential energy of **9 J** at the top of its flight.

Assume that there's no air resistance.

a) What is the ball's **kinetic energy** just before it hits the ground? Tick the box next to the correct answer.

☐ 0 J   ☐ 9 J   ☐ 81 J

b) Explain your answer to part **a)**.

....

....

Q2 A roller coaster and passengers are **stationary** at the top of a ride. At this point they have a gravitational potential energy of **300 kJ**.

a) Draw lines to connect the correct energy statement with each stage of the roller coaster.

A — minimum G.P.E., maximum K.E.
B — K.E. is being converted to G.P.E.
C — G.P.E. is being converted to K.E.
D — maximum G.P.E.

K.E. = Kinetic energy
G.P.E. = gravitational potential energy

b) i) When the roller coaster is at **half** its original height, how much kinetic energy should it have?

....

ii) Explain why in real life the kinetic energy is **less** than this.

....

Q3 Jo is sitting at the top of a helter-skelter ride. Her mass is **50 kg**.

G.P.E. = mass × g × height

a) At the top of the helter-skelter, Jo is **8 m** above the ground. What is her change in gravitational potential energy as she slides down to the bottom? (g = 10 m/s²)

....

....

b) At the bottom her kinetic energy is **1500 J**. How much energy has been '**wasted**' coming down the ride?

....

c) Which **force** causes this energy to be wasted? Circle the answer.

friction   gravity   thrust

Module P3 — Forces for Transport

Fuel Consumption and Emissions

Q1 Complete this passage using the words in the box.

more higher smaller size larger less design lower

A car's power rating depends on the .... and ....
of the engine. The .... or more powerful an engine, the
.... energy it transfers from its fuel every second.
This means it usually has a .... fuel consumption.

You won't need to use all the words.

Q2 A car's fuel consumption is **3.4 l/100 km**. How much fuel is used in a **200 km** journey? Tick the box next to the answer.

☐ 3.4 l   ☐ 8.5 l   ☐ 6.8 l   ☐ 10.0 l

Q3 Tick the boxes next to the things that **increase** a car's fuel consumption.

Adding a roof box to the car. ☐

Making the car more streamlined. ☐

Adding deflectors. ☐

Winding down the windows. ☐

Q4 The table below shows data on **CO_2 emissions** and **fuel consumption** for four different cars.

Car	CO_2 Emissions (g/km)	Fuel Consumption (l/100 km)
Trygve XXL	139	5.6
Waldheim 4.1	345	12.4
Boutros GTI	227	8.4
Annan 97eco	181	5.2

a) Which car would you expect to be the most expensive to run? ....

b) Circle the correct word to complete the sentence in the box.

In general the higher the fuel consumption, the **greater** / **lower** the emissions.

Module P3 — Forces for Transport

Fuels for Cars

Q1 Tick the boxes to show whether the following statements are **true** or **false**.

		True	False
a)	Biofuels can be used instead of fossil fuels in cars.	☐	☐
b)	Biofuels are non-renewable.	☐	☐
c)	Burning biofuels produces more pollution overall that burning fossil fuels.	☐	☐

Q2 Petrol is made from oil, which is a **fossil fuel**.

a) Are fossil fuels renewable or non-renewable?
....

b) Give two **environmental problems** that burning fossil fuels in cars can cause.

1. ....

2. ....

c) Give an example of a fuel you could use **instead** of fossil fuels. ....

Q3 Trevor's car has **two engines**, a normal **petrol** engine and an **electric** motor. He uses the electric motor for short journeys but uses the petrol engine for longer drives.

a) Explain how using the electric motor causes less damage to the environment **whilst driving**.

....

....

b) Explain why using the electric motor can still cause damage to the environment.

....

....

....

c) Why does Trevor have to use the **petrol** engine for longer journeys? Circle the answer.

The electric motor has to be plugged into the mains at all times.	The petrol engine won't harm the environment as much on longer journeys.	The electric motor can only drive the car a certain distance before the batteries have to be recharged.

d) Trevor fits his car with solar panels so he can charge the batteries using energy from the Sun. Give **one advantage** and **one disadvantage** of using solar panels to provide electricity.

Advantage: ....

Disadvantage: ....

Module P3 — Forces for Transport

Mixed Questions — Module P3

Q1 Three hockey players are practising for a match. They each push the hockey ball as hard as they can.

Think about what two things she would need to measure, and the calculation she should use.

a) Suggest how a player could find out the average speed of her ball.

....

b) The force with which each player pushes the hockey ball is shown in the diagram below. Which player would you expect to give the ball the greatest acceleration? Explain your answer.

player A — 60 N
player B — 80 N
player C — 100 N

....

Q2 The graph shows Mr Alonso's speed as he drives down a hill.

a) His car is accelerating. How can you tell this from the graph?

....

b) His car reaches the bottom of the hill after **6 s**. What was his increase in speed down the hill?

....

c) Use your answer to part **b)** to calculate the **acceleration** of the car down the hill.

....

d) Explain how a **seat belt** would help keep Mr Alonso safer in a crash.

....

e) Circle the correct word in each pair to complete the sentences on Mr Alonso's fuel consumption.

> Winding down the windows will **increase** / **decrease** Mr. Alonso's fuel consumption. This is because it will **increase** / **decrease** the air resistance and so **less** / **more** fuel is needed to do work against it.

Module P3 — Forces for Transport

Mixed Questions — Module P3

Q3 Cherie and Tony rob a bank. They escape in their getaway car and drive at a constant speed on a straight road.

   a) Are the forces on the getaway car balanced or unbalanced?

   ....

   b) While she's driving, Cherie is distracted looking out for the police.

   How is this likely to affect her **thinking distance**?

   ....

   c) A police car swings into the road just ahead of Cherie, forcing her to slam on her brakes. Tick the boxes next to the things that could **increase** her braking distance.

   ☐ A wet road.   ☐ A heavier loot.   ☐ A slower speed.   ☐ New tyres.

Q4 Humphrey is working in a supermarket stocking shelves with cans of baked beans. Each can weighs **5 N**.

work done = force × distance

   a) He lifts the cans onto a shelf **1.8 m** high.
   How much work does he do lifting one can from the floor onto the shelf?

   ....

   ....

   b) One of the cans falls off the shelf.
   What is the kinetic energy of the can just before it hits the floor? Circle the answer.

       18 J   **9 J**

               81 J   **0 J**

   c) Humphrey shows off by putting **32** cans on the shelf in **60** seconds. Calculate his **power**.

   power = work done ÷ time taken

   ....

   ....

Module P3 — Forces for Transport

Mixed Questions — Module P3

Q5 Norman loves trainspotting. As a special treat, he plots a **distance-time** graph for two of the trains.

  a) For how long is train 2 stationary?

  ....

  b) Both trains start at a steady speed. How do we know this?

  ....

  c) Describe the motion of train 1 between 40 s and 80 s.

  ....

  ....

Q6 Jane is carrying out a science experiment at school. She drops a table tennis ball from a window on the top floor. At first the ball **accelerates**, but it soon reaches a **steady speed**.

  a) Explain why the table tennis ball accelerates at first.

  ....

  ....

  b) Explain why the table tennis ball reaches a steady speed.

  ....

  ....

  ....

  c) Jane measures the time taken for the ball to hit the ground. She repeats the experiment several times and obtains the results below.

          2.86 s   3.10 s   2.95 s   3.00 s

  i) Which time gives the greatest speed for the falling table tennis ball? ....

  ii) Calculate the average time taken for the ball to hit the ground.

  ....

  iii) Suggest why Jane repeated her experiment several times.

  ....

  d) The ball bounces upwards after hitting the ground. What **force** causes the ball to bounce? Circle the answer.

      gravity   the friction from the ground   air resistance   the reaction force from the ground

Module P3 — Forces for Transport

Module B4 — It's a Green World

Collecting Methods

Q1 Draw lines to match each word to the correct definition.

Population — Groups of different species living in an area.

Community — All the organisms of one species living in an area.

Q2 Laura and Claire want to study the population of beetles in their back garden. They both want to use different methods to count the beetles.

Laura: I want to collect beetles by letting them fall into a trap which they can't get out of.

Claire: I want to suck up individual beetles through a collection tube.

a) Which collection methods are Laura and Claire thinking of using?

Laura .... Claire ....

b) Next, Laura and Claire want to collect **butterflies**. Describe a method they could use to do this.

....

....

Top Tips: There are loads of methods for collecting organisms and it can be easy to get them mixed up. Make sure you know the difference between pooters, nets and pitfall traps for the exam — and that you can describe how each one works. It's an easy way to collect marks.

Counting and Identifying Organisms

Q1 Mark wants to know what types of plants and animals live in his garden. He decides to study a **1 m² area** of his garden in detail, using a **quadrat**.

a) What is a **quadrat**? Circle the correct answer below.

    a magnifying glass   a square frame enclosing a known area   a small jar enclosing an unknown area

b) Describe what Mark could do to show that a variety of plants and animals live in a small area of his garden.

....

....

c) Mark finds it hard to count all the individual grass plants in the quadrat. Suggest what he could do to avoid this problem.

....

....

d) Mark finds two types of plant that he doesn't recognise. Use the key to **identify** the plants from the samples shown below.

1.	Does the plant have seeds?	Yes – go to 2. No – go to 3.
2.	Does the plant have flowers?	Yes – it is a flowering plant. No – it is a conifer.
3.	Does the plant have long stems with lots of small leaves?	Yes – it is a fern. No – it is a moss.

i) Type of plant: ....

ii) Type of plant: ....

Module B4 — It's a Green World

Estimating Population Sizes

Q1 Some students wanted to estimate the size of the population of plants in their school field. They counted the number of clover plants, daisies and dandelions in a **1 m² quadrat**. Their results are shown in the table below.

	Clover Plants	Daisies	Dandelions
Number of plants in 1 m²	11	9	4
Estimate of number of plants in whole school field	11 × 45 = 495		

a) The area of the whole school field is **45 m²**. Complete the table by estimating the number of each plant in the whole school field. The first one has been done for you.

b) How can this method of estimating a population best be described? Circle the answer below.

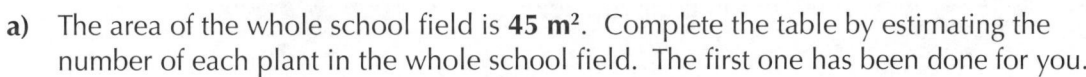

Q2 Michael carried out a **capture-recapture** experiment. His data is shown below.

- There were **30** crickets caught and marked in the first sample.
- There were **30** crickets caught in the second sample.
- **6** of the crickets in the second sample were marked.

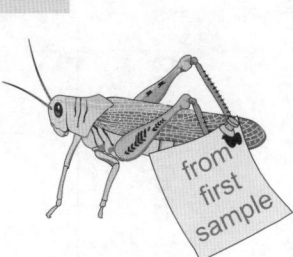

Estimate the population size using the formula in the box below.

$$\text{Population Size} = \frac{\text{number in first sample} \times \text{number in second sample}}{\text{number in second sample previously marked}}$$

....

....

Top Tips: The equation might look big and tough but it's really not that bad. Read it carefully, find the right numbers you need from the data you're given and you'll be fine. You might even be estimating population sizes for fun on a Saturday night soon... or not.

Module B4 — It's a Green World

Ecosystems and Distribution of Organisms

Q1 a) Circle the correct definition of the word '**ecosystem**' from the choices below.

> The place where an organism lives.

> All the organisms living in a particular area.

> All the organisms living in a particular area, as well as all the non-living conditions.

b) Explain the difference between a **habitat** and an **ecosystem**.

....

....

Q2 Taylor is studying the distribution of two plant species across the school playground.

a) Number the steps **1** to **3** to show how he could carry out a **transect** to help with his investigation.

☐ Place quadrats next to each other all the way along the line.

☐ Mark out a line using a tape measure.

☐ Write down the number of plant species found in each quadrat.

Taylor draws the following kite diagram from the results of his transect:

b) i) Where did Taylor find **species 1** along the transect line?

....

ii) Where did Taylor find the most of **species 2** along the transect line?

....

Module B4 — It's a Green World

Distribution of Organisms

Q1 The distribution of organisms can be affected by **physical factors**.

a) What is meant by the term '**physical factors**'? Tick the correct answer.

- Other organisms living in the area and sharing resources. ☐
- The plants and animals available as food. ☐
- Non-living things like light, temperature, water and oxygen. ☐

b) Explain how physical factors affect the distribution of organisms.

....

....

....

Remember: distribution means where something is found.

Q2 The distribution of organisms can be affected by **other organisms** in the habitat.

a) Foxes like to eat rabbits.
Suggest how this may affect the **distribution** of:

i) the rabbits in an area.

....

....

ii) foxes in the same area.

....

b) Describe **one** other way in which an organism's distribution can be affected by **another living organism**.

....

....

Top Tips: When we're choosing where to live we might look for somewhere with a sea-view, a big garden and a chip shop nearby. But there are none of these decisions for plants and animals. They basically just want somewhere where they have the best chance of surviving.

Module B4 — It's a Green World

Biodiversity

Q1 What does the word '**biodiversity**' mean? Circle the correct answer below.

The variety of characteristics seen in different species.

The way species have changed through evolution.

The variety of different species living in a habitat.

Q2 There are **natural** and **artificial** ecosystems.

Draw lines to match each ecosystem to the correct description and example.

Ecosystem	Description	Example
natural ecosystem	looks after itself without any help from humans	forestry plantation
artificial ecosystem	created and looked after by humans	native woodland

Q3 The table below shows data for a fish farm and a natural lake.

	Fish Farm	Natural Lake
Number of fish	10 000	3 000
Number of different fish species	1	15
Number of other animal species	3	50
Number of different plant species	10	50

a) Is a fish farm a **natural** ecosystem or an **artificial** ecosystem?

....

b) i) Which ecosystem has the highest **biodiversity** — the fish farm or the natural lake?

....

ii) Explain your answer to part **i**).

....

....

Module B4 — It's a Green World

Plants and Photosynthesis

Q1 a) Circle the correct **word equation** for photosynthesis below.

carbon dioxide + water →[LIGHT / chlorophyll]→ glucose + oxygen

carbon dioxide + glucose →[LIGHT / chlorophyll]→ water + oxygen

water + oxygen →[LIGHT / chlorophyll]→ glucose + carbon dioxide

b) Complete the **chemical equation** for photosynthesis using the chemical symbols from the box. One has been done for you.

$6CO_2$ $C_6H_{12}O_6$ $6O_2$ $6H_2O$

.... + ... →[LIGHT / chlorophyll]→ $C_6H_{12}O_6$ + ...

c) "Oxygen is a **waste product** of photosynthesis." Is this **true** or **false**? ....

Q2 Some plant cells contain **chloroplasts**.

a) What takes place in the chloroplasts? Underline the correct answer below.

respiration   photosynthesis   protein synthesis

b) Not all plant cells have chloroplasts. Explain why this is.

....

Q3 a) Circle the correct word in each pair to complete the sentences.

i) More carbon dioxide will make a plant photosynthesise **slower / faster**.

ii) **More / Less** light will make a plant photosynthesise faster.

iii) A low temperature will make a plant photosynthesise **faster / slower**.

iv) The faster a plant can photosynthesise, the **slower / faster** it will grow.

b) Plants grow faster in the summer. Explain why this happens.

....

....

....

Module B4 — It's a Green World

More on Photosynthesis

Q1 Circle the correct word from each pair to complete the following sentences.

> In plants, glucose is usually stored as **glucose** / **starch**.
> It's transported as **soluble sugars** / **starch**.

Q2 a) Glucose is '**soluble**'. What does this mean? Underline the correct answer below.

- Glucose won't mix with water.
- Glucose will dissolve in water.
- Glucose will react with water.
- Glucose is sweet.

b) Is **starch** soluble or insoluble?

....

Q3 Complete the passage about **glucose** by choosing the correct words from the list below.

| converted | growth | repair | cellulose | energy |

Plants make glucose in their leaves. Some of the glucose is used for respiration, which releases .... This means the rest of the glucose can be .... into other useful substances. Glucose can be converted to .... for making cell walls. Glucose is also used to make proteins. These are needed for .... and ....

Q4 Glucose can be converted to other substances for **storage**.
Circle **two** of these substances from the ones below.

Module B4 — It's a Green World

Understanding Photosynthesis

Q1 How did **early Greek scientists** think plants gained mass? Circle the correct answer below.

- by taking in minerals from the soil
- by storing glucose as starch
- by taking in water from the soil

Q2 **Van Helmont** carried out an experiment to investigate how plants gain mass. He planted a willow tree in some soil and left it for 5 years, adding only water to the soil.

a) When van Helmont weighed the **tree** after 5 years its mass had increased. What happened to the mass of the **soil**? Circle the correct answer.

- It increased.
- It stayed the same.
- It decreased.

b) What conclusions can be drawn from van Helmont's results? Tick **two** answers.

☐ The tree had gained mass from something other than minerals in the soil.

☐ The tree had only gained mass by taking in minerals from the soil.

☐ The tree had gained mass by taking in water.

Q3 Miss Webb's biology class are recreating some of **Priestley's** famous experiments.

a) They place a lit candle in a sealed container and leave it until it goes out. What you would expect to happen when they try to re-light the candle in the sealed container? Circle the correct answer.

The candle will re-light.   **The candle won't re-light.**

b) The class carry out the experiment again. This time they place a **green plant** in the container along with the candle. What do you think will happen when they try to re-light the candle in a week's time? Circle the correct answer.

The candle will re-light.   **The candle won't re-light.**

c) After his experiment, Priestly concluded that plants must put something back in the air that a burning candle takes out. What is this substance?

....

Module B4 — It's a Green World

Diffusion

Q1 Circle the correct words in the sentences below.

> Diffusion is the net movement of particles from an area of **higher** / **lower** concentration to an area of **higher** / **lower** concentration. Diffusion happens in substances where **individual** / **groups of** particles are free to move about in **an organised** / **a random** way.

Q2 The first diagram below shows a **cup of water** which has just had a **drop of dye** added.

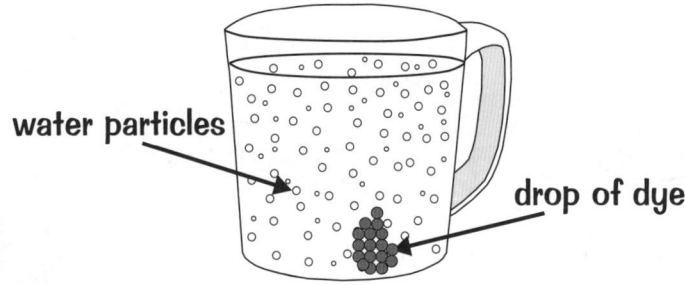 

a) In the second cup above, draw how the molecules of **dye** will look in the water after an hour.

b) Explain the movement of the dye particles.
You'll need to talk about **concentration** in your answer.

....

....

Q3 Diffusion happens across **cell membranes**.

Look at the two diagrams below.

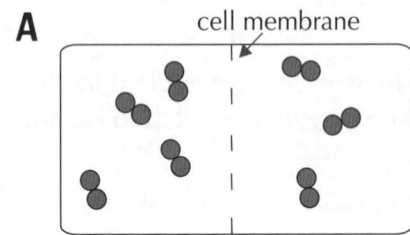 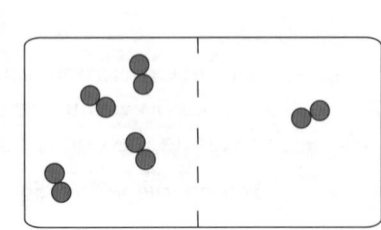

In each case, would you expect there to be a movement of particles from right to left, or from left to right?

A .... B ....

Module B4 — It's a Green World

Diffusion

Q4 Tick the boxes to show whether the following statements about diffusion are **true** or **false**.

		True	False
a)	Substances move out of a cell by diffusion.	☐	☐
b)	Substances can't enter a cell by diffusion.	☐	☐
c)	Diffusion happens across cell walls.	☐	☐
d)	Only small molecules can fit through a cell membrane.	☐	☐

Q5 Phil was investigating the diffusion of **glucose** and **starch** through a **membrane**. He placed equal amounts of glucose solution and starch solution inside a bag designed to act like a cell membrane. He then put the bag into a beaker of water.

a) At the beginning of the experiment, which area had the highest concentration of glucose and starch? Circle the correct answer below.

   the water   the 'cell membrane' bag

b) After an hour, Phil tested the water for the presence of starch and glucose. Circle which one of the following you would expect to be found in the water outside the bag:

   glucose   starch

   Starch molecules are bigger than glucose molecules.

c) Explain your answer to part **b)**.

   ....

   ....

   ....

Module B4 — It's a Green World

Leaves and Diffusion

Q1 Plants carry out both **photosynthesis** and **respiration**.

a) Why do plants carry out **respiration**? Circle the correct answer below.

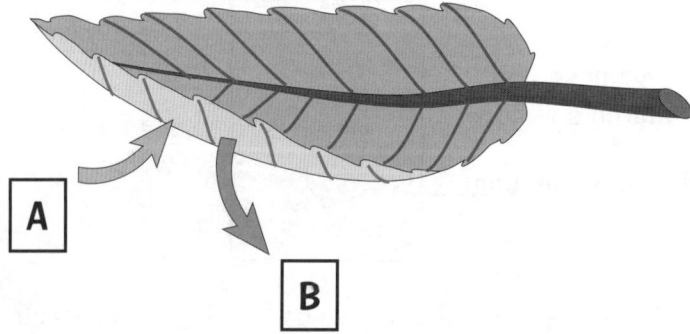

b) When does respiration in plants take place? Circle the correct answer below.

only during the day   only at night   all the time

Q2 The diagram shows a leaf which is **photosynthesising**.

a) i) On the diagram, which arrow shows the movement of **oxygen**?

....

ii) Which arrow shows the movement of **carbon dioxide**?

....

b) Explain your answer to part **a) ii)**.

Talk about diffusion in your answer.

....

....

....

Top Tips: Yep, I'm sorry to say there's more than just photosynthesis to think about when it comes to plants — there's respiration as well. It's not too tricky though, you've just got to figure out which way oxygen and carbon dioxide are going for each process.

Module B4 — It's a Green World

Leaves and Photosynthesis

Q1 a) Name the parts labelled **A – E** to complete the diagram of a **leaf** below.

A ....
....
C ....
B ....
E ....
D ....

b) Name the part of the leaf that **carbon dioxide** enters through.

....

c) Name the part of the leaf that **oxygen** leaves through.

....

Q2 Draw lines to match up the following **features** of a leaf with how they help with **photosynthesis**.

chlorophyll and other pigments	transport water and nutrients and support the leaf
vascular bundles	absorb light energy from different parts of the spectrum
thin leaves	control when stomata open and close
guard cells	short diffusion distance

Q3 Most plants have **broad leaves**. Give two ways in which this feature helps the plant during photosynthesis.

1. ....

....

2. ....

....

Module B4 — It's a Green World

Osmosis

Q1 Fill in the gaps in the passage below using the words in the box.

| diffusion | partially | water | lower | higher |

Osmosis is the movement of .... molecules across a .... permeable membrane from a region of .... water concentration to a region of .... water concentration.

Osmosis is a special type of ....

Q2 Osmosis is similar to diffusion. Tick the sentence below which is true for **both osmosis** and **diffusion**.

The process only happens across a membrane. ☐

Molecules move from an area of higher concentration to an area of lower concentration. ☐

Only water molecules move in the process. ☐

Learning by osmosis

Q3 Look at the diagram and answer the questions below.

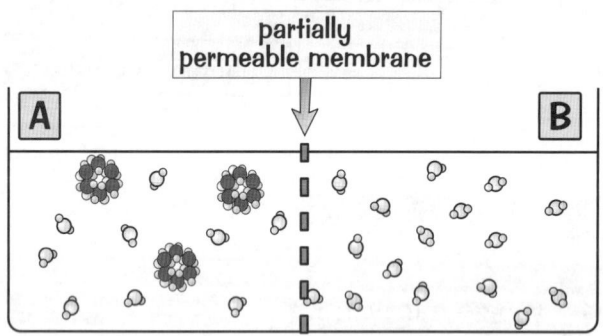

- Water molecule
- Glucose molecule

a) What is a partially permeable membrane? Circle the correct answer below.

A membrane with big holes in it.

A membrane with no holes in it.　　　A membrane with tiny holes in it.

b) On which side of the membrane is there the highest concentration of **water molecules**?

....

Module B4 — It's a Green World

Osmosis

Q4 Circle the correct words in each pair to complete the passage below.

> Water moves in and out of plant and animal cells by **osmosis / diffusion** through the cell **wall / membrane**. When a plant is **well / not** watered the contents of the cells push against the **elastic / inelastic** cell wall. This is called **turgor / tissue** pressure and it helps to **repair / support** the plant tissues.

Q5 Archie's mum asked him to water her prized plant collection while she was away on holiday for a week. Unfortunately, Archie forgot.

a) What is likely to happen to the plants after a week without water?

....

b) Explain your answer to part **a)**.

....

....

....

Q6 It's important that the amount of **water** in **animal cells** is carefully controlled.

a) Describe what happens to an animal cell if it **takes in** too much water.

....

b) Describe what happens to an animal cell if it **loses** too much water.

....

Top Tips: Osmosis sounds scary, but it's really just a fancy sort of diffusion. Not only is it important for getting water in and out of both plant and animal cells, it could come up in the exam. So don't wait for this stuff to diffuse into your brain — learn how it works.

Module B4 — It's a Green World

Transport Systems in Plants

Q1 Put the following statements under the **correct heading** in the table. One's been done for you.

~~transport substances up the stem~~
transport minerals
transport substances both up and down the stem
transport food substances
transport water

Xylem vessels	Phloem vessels
transport substances up the stem	

Q2 Draw lines to match each vessel to the way it moves substances and where it moves them to.

xylem   translocation   growing and storage tissues

phloem   transpiration   shoot and leaves

Q3 The diagram shows a cross-section of a **leaf**.

a) Label a **xylem vessel**, and a **phloem vessel** on the diagram.

b) Circle a **vascular bundle** on the diagram.

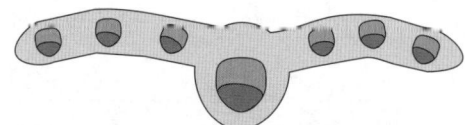

Q4 The diagram shows a cross-section of a **plant's stem**.

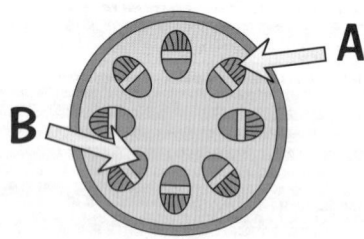

a) Name parts A and B.

A = ...

B = ...

b) Describe the function of **A** in the stem.

....

c) Describe one way that a cross-section of a **root** would look different from the cross-section of a stem.

....

Module B4 — It's a Green World

Water Flow Through Plants

Q1 Complete this diagram of a **plant** according to the instructions given below.

a) Put an **X** on the diagram to show one place where water enters the plant.

b) Add a **Y** to the diagram to show one place where water leaves the plant.

c) Add arrows to the diagram to show how water moves from where it enters to where it leaves.

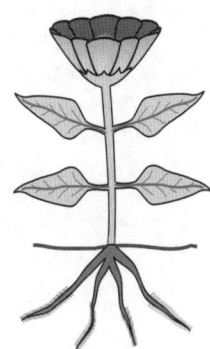

Q2 Choose from the following words to complete the passage.

leaves	evaporation	transpiration	roots	xylem	stem

Most water leaves plants through the .... by ....
and diffusion of water vapour. This creates a slight shortage of water in the
.............................., which draws water from the rest of the plant through the
.... vessels. This causes more water to be drawn up from the
.... This whole process is called ....

Q3 Give two ways that transpiration **benefits** plants.

1. ....

2. ....

Q4 a) Draw a diagram of a **root hair cell** in the box provided.

b) Describe how water is drawn into this cell.

....

....

Q5 Circle the correct words to complete the paragraph.

To reduce water loss, leaves can have a **waxy** / **spongy** cuticle covering the epidermis. This helps make the upper surface of the leaf **waterproof** / **soft**. Most stomata are found on the **under** / **upper** side of the leaf where it's darker and cooler. This helps **slow down** / **speed up** diffusion of water out of the leaf. **A healthy** / **An unhealthy** plant balances water loss with water uptake.

Module B4 — It's a Green World

Water Flow Through Plants

Q6 Ben wants to measure the **transpiration rate** of a plant. Describe a method he could use to do this.

....

....

....

....

Q7 The **rate of transpiration** is affected by different factors. From each pair of plants, circle the letter next to the plant that will **lose water faster**. Give reasons for your choices.

Assume all other factors are identical.

a) A — in a dark cupboard   B — on a windowsill

Reason: ....

b) A — in a warm cupboard   B — in a fridge

Reason: ....

c) A — in a cupboard   B — with a fan

Reason: ....

d) A — in a polythene bag   B — in an airy room

The polythene bag traps moisture in the air.

Reason: ....

Module B4 — It's a Green World

Minerals Needed for Healthy Growth

Q1 Draw lines to match the following **minerals** with what they're need for in plants. One's been done for you.

MAGNESIUM	for making proteins for cell growth
NITRATES	for photosynthesis
PHOSPHATES	for respiration and growth
POTASSIUM	for photosynthesis and respiration

Q2 Tick the boxes to show if the following statements are **true** or **false**.

   True   False

a) Minerals are absorbed by root hairs. ☐ ☐

b) Minerals are absorbed from the soil ☐ ☐

c) The concentration of minerals in soil is usually high. ☐ ☐

d) Minerals absorbed from the soil are dissolved in solution. ☐ ☐

Q3 Spring has arrived but Pat has noticed that his **cabbages** are **not** growing well and the plants have yellow older leaves.

a) Suggest a cause of both the poor plant growth and yellow older leaves.

....

Pat has been offered some **manure** for his field.
The table shows the mineral content of different manures.

Material	% Nitrogen	% Phosphorus	% Potassium
Horse manure	0.6	0.1	0.5
Pig manure	0.4	0.1	0.5
Poultry manure	1.0	0.4	0.6
Sheep manure	0.8	0.1	0.7

b) Which type of manure would you recommend Pat use? Explain your answer.

....

....

Module B4 — It's a Green World

More on Minerals

Q1 An investigation into the **mineral requirements** of plants was carried out as shown below.

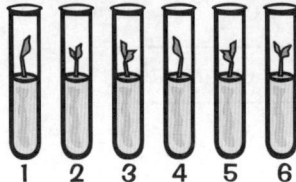

tubes 1 and 2: complete mineral supply
tubes 3 and 4: deficient in phosphates
tubes 5 and 6: deficient in magnesium

a) The plants were grown a solutions of nutrients rather than soil.
Fill in the blank to show what this is called.

.... culture

b) Suggest why tubes 1 and 2 were included.

....

c) Suggest why enough of all the minerals except one was supplied to tubes 3, 4, 5 and 6.

....

....

Q2 **Fertilisers** are often added to the soil to make plants and crops grow better.

a) Most fertilisers are given a NPK value. What do the letters NPK refer to?
Underline the correct answer below.

nitrates, phosphates and potassium

nitrates, phosphates and magnesium   nitrates, potassium and copper

b) Write the letter of the bag of fertiliser that contains the highest proportion of:

i) nitrates. ....

ii) potassium. ....

A — NPK value: 25-12-8
B — NPK value: 8-12-30
C — NPK value: 15-30-15

c) What other mineral may be included in fertilisers in small quantities?

....

Top Tip: Plants are fussy things. Don't give them enough of what they want and they just won't grow properly. Lucky there's all this fertiliser made to give them just what they need. Although I don't think they'd be so keen if they had noses and could actually smell the stuff.

Decay

Q1 a) Why is **decay** important to **plants**? Circle the correct word in each pair to complete the sentence.

Decay releases the **oxygen** / **minerals** which plants need for **growth** / **photosynthesis**.

b) What name is given to microorganisms that cause decay? Underline the correct answer below.

decomposers   **parasites**   **pests**

c) Name the type of waste (**plant** or **human**) that microorganisms decay in the following places:

i) sewage works ....   ii) compost heaps ....

Q2 The **rate of decay** depends on several things.

a) Circle the correct graph below which shows the effect **oxygen** has on the rate of decay.

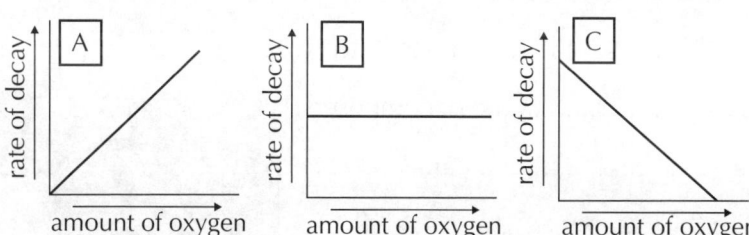

b) Give another two factors that will affect the rate of decay.

1. ....

2. ....

Q3 Broth was boiled in flasks A and B below. The broth was then allowed to cool and left for a few days. The broth in one of the flasks **decayed**.

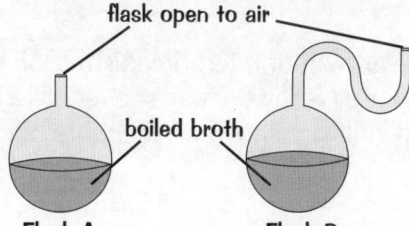

a) In which flask did the broth decay? ....

b) Name two types of microorganism that may have caused the broth to decay.

1. .... 2. ....

c) Explain how the **shape** of the flasks affected which broth decayed and which stayed fresh.

....

....

Q4 Use the words provided to fill in the gaps in the paragraph below.

.... are a type of decomposer. They include earthworms, maggots and .... They feed on dead and decaying material known as .... As they do this, they increase the .... of the material, which helps other decomposers to digest it.

surface area
detritivores
woodlice
detritus

Module B4 — It's a Green World

Preventing Decay

Q1 Draw lines to link the **food preservation methods** with how they reduce decay.

- Drying — acidic environment kills decomposers
- Adding vinegar — decomposers can't reproduce at such low temperatures
- Freezing — decomposers need water, so can't survive

Q2 **Tuna** is often stored in **brine** (salt water) in a can.

a) Fill in the gaps to explain how canning tuna in this way can prevent decay.

| lose | sealed | decomposers | kills |

Tuna is put into salt water. This causes the decomposers to .... water by osmosis. This .... the decomposers. The tuna is then put into a .... can. This keeps the .... out.

b) Suggest **one** other substance which would have the same effect on decomposers as salt water.

....

Q3 Beth was investigating the effect of **temperature** on the growth of microorganisms. She left three identical slices of bread in different temperatures for four days. Every day she recorded what percentage of each slice was covered in mould. Her results are shown in the table below.

Temp (°C)	Percentage of Mould Cover (%)			
	Day 1	Day 2	Day 3	Day 4
0	0	0	0	1
20	2	6	12	24
40	5	15	30	40

a) Draw a line graph on the grid provided to show the results for **day 4**.

b) What effect does temperature have on the rate of decay?

....

c) Suggest why some food is often kept in the fridge.

....

Intensive Farming

Q1 What does **intensive farming** mean? Tick the correct answer.

☐ Having as many farmers working on the farm as possible.

☐ Trying to produce as much food as possible from the land, plants and animals available.

☐ Carrying out continuous farming activities from dusk till dawn.

Q2 Complete the sentences to describe how intensive farming methods can **increase productivity**.

photosynthesis   predators   nutrient   tanks   soil   controlled   barren
Fish farming involves rearing fish in .... or fenced-off areas of water.
This protects them from ....
By growing plants in glasshouses, the conditions can be ....
to increase the rate of ....
Hydroponics is a method of growing food using .... solutions instead of
.... This method can be used in areas with .... soil.

Q3 The table below shows the percentages of the egg market shared by three methods of chicken farming — **battery farm**, **barn** and **free range**.

Year	Percentage of egg market for each type of chicken farming		
	Battery	Barn	Free range
1999	78	6	16
2001	72	5	23
2003	69	6	25
2005	66	7	27

a) Which type of farm has the highest **productivity**?

....

b) Suggest why some people are **against** intensive farming methods such as battery farming.

....

....

Module B4 — It's a Green World

Intensive Farming

Q4 The graph shows how much wheat Mr Moore's farm produced over 4 different years. One year he didn't use any pesticides, and in the other three years he used pesticides.

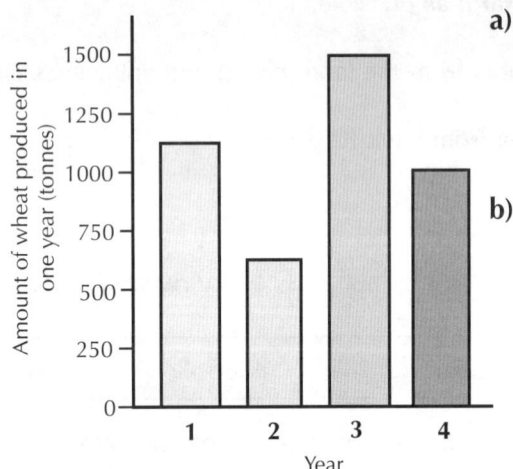

a) Pesticides kill pests. What are **pests**? Circle the correct answer below.

Any organisms that live in the same habitat as crops.   Any organisms that damage crops.

b) i) Look at the graph. In which year is it most likely that Mr Moore didn't use any pesticides?

....

ii) Explain your answer to part **i**).

....

c) Fill in the spaces to give examples of the types of pesticides that Mr Moore may have used and what each one is used to kill. One has been done for you.

......*insecticides*...... to kill ......*insects*......

.... to kill ....

.... to kill ....

Q5 **Intensive farming** has many **disadvantages**.

a) Use the words in the box to complete the passage.

| humans | accumulate | persistent | pests |

Pesticides may kill organisms which aren't ....

Some pesticides are ...., which means they're hard to get rid of.

Pesticides can also .... (build up) in food chains. This can kill animals further up the food chain. A build up of pesticides in the food chain could also cause health risks for ....

b) Other than the effect on food chains, describe one **negative** effect that intensive farming can have on the environment.

....

....

Module B4 — It's a Green World

More on Farming

Q1 Biological control is an alternative to using pesticides.

a) What is biological control? Underline the correct answer.

Using living things instead of chemicals to control a pest.

Letting nature control itself with no human input.

b) Complete the table by giving two advantages and two disadvantages of using **predators** to control pests.

Advantages	Disadvantages
1.	1.
2.	2.

Q2 a) Use the words in the box to complete the passage about **organic farming**.

weeding	manure	fertilisers	compost	planting

Organic farming doesn't use artificial .... or chemical pesticides.
There are many different techniques involved in organic farming. For example, using
animal .... and .... adds nutrients to the soil.
.... involves pulling out weeds rather than using a herbicide.
Farmers may also vary seed .... times in order to avoid major pests.

b) Explain **one** advantage and **one** disadvantage of organic farming.

Advantage: ....

Disadvantage: ....

Q3 **Cockroaches** were sprayed with a **pesticide** to control the size of their population.

Explain what effect this could have on the rest of the food web shown.

....

....

....

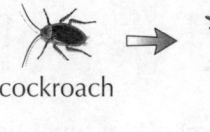
cockroach   frog

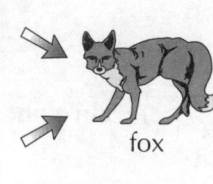
rabbit   fox

Module B4 — It's a Green World

Mixed Questions — Module B4

Q1 Farmer MacDonald puts **fertiliser** on his crops. The fertiliser he uses provides the crops with essential minerals to ensure healthy growth.

   a) Which minerals are most important for photosynthesis? Circle **two** answers.

   nitrates   phosphates   magnesium   potassium

   b) Which mineral is vital for making proteins? ....

   c) Describe the symptoms of a plant with:

   i) **potassium** deficiency.

   ....

   ii) **magnesium** deficiency.

   ....

   d) Farmer MacDonald is thinking of trying some organic farming methods. Explain how he could use crop rotation and nitrogen fixing crops instead of fertilisers and pesticides.

   ....

   ....

   ....

   ....

Q2 The diagram below shows a cross-section through a **plant root**.

   a) Draw arrows to link up each label to the correct part of the root.

   phloem   root hair

   xylem

   b) Root hairs are important for absorbing water needed to keep the plant healthy. By what process does water move into the root hair cells? Circle the answer.

   osmosis   diffusion   transpiration

   c) Give **one** other important function of root hairs.

   ....

Module B4 — It's a Green World

Mixed Questions — Module B4

Q3 Sally is growing some **tomato plants** in her **greenhouse**, but they aren't growing very quickly and some of them have died.

a) The greenhouse already has lots of light. What other substances do the tomato plant need in order to carry out **photosynthesis**? Circle **two** answers.

   nitrogen   fertiliser   carbon dioxide   water

b) Sally finds some insects on her tomatoes. Suggest two ways she could deal with these **pests**.

   1. ....

   2. ....

c) Sally puts her dead tomato plants in a **composter**. What organisms break down the plant material?

   ....

d) Sally decides to use **hydroponics** to grow her tomatoes.

   i) Is this an **intensive farming** or **organic** method?

   ....

   ii) What is hydroponics?

   ....

Q4 Eric wants to catch some of the ladybird population in his garden so he can study them.

a) What is a population?

   ....

b) Describe two methods he could use to catch ladybirds.

   1. ....

   2. ....

c) Eric decides he wants to estimate the population size of ladybirds in his garden. Explain how he could do this by scaling up from a small sample area.

   ....

   ....

   ....

Module B4 — It's a Green World

Module C4 — The Periodic Table

The History of the Atom

Q1 The theory of **atomic structure** has changed over the past two hundred years. Draw lines to put these theories on the time line in the **correct order**.

beginning of the 19th century → present day

- J J Thomson's positive sphere with electrons in it.
- Bohr's electron shell theory.
- Dalton's solid spheres.
- Rutherford's theory of the nuclear atom.

Q2 Which of the diagrams below show **Rutherford's** idea of the **atom**? Circle the answer.

A — positively charged ball / electrons

B — nucleus / electrons / empty space

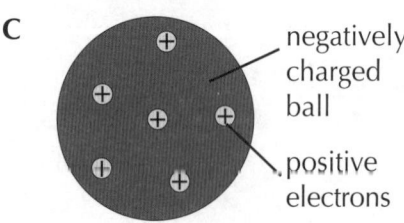

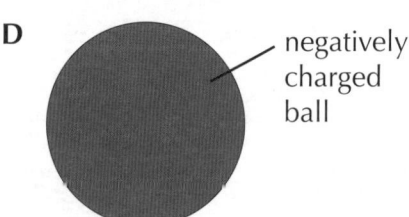

C — negatively charged ball / positive electrons

D — negatively charged ball

Q3 Lots of different scientists have worked on the model of the **atom**.

a) Tick the box next to the name of the scientist who discovered that atoms contain electrons.

☐ J J Thomson
☐ Bohr
☐ Dalton
☐ Rutherford

b) Bohr's model was different to previous theories. Circle the statement that best describes Bohr's model.

Electrons can only exist in orbits, or shells around the nucleus.

Negative electrons are scattered around the nucleus.

Different solid balls make up the different elements.

Atoms

Q1 All substances are made up of **atoms**. Atoms are made up of smaller parts.

Tick the boxes below to show whether each sentence is **true** or **false**.

		True	False
a)	Electrons are positively charged.	☐	☐
b)	The nucleus contains protons and electrons.	☐	☐
c)	Electrons have very little mass.	☐	☐
d)	The nucleus has a positive charge.	☐	☐
e)	Electrons are tiny.	☐	☐
f)	Atoms have small mass but a large size.	☐	☐

Q2 Circle the sentence below that is **true** for **atoms**.

atoms have a charge of +1

atoms have a charge of 0

atoms have a charge of −1

Q3 Complete this table.

Particle	Mass	Charge
	1	+1
Neutron	1	
Electron		−1

Q4 This question is about an atom of **magnesium**.

An atom of magnesium can be represented by the following symbol: $^{24}_{12}Mg$

a) What is the **mass number** of this atom?

....

b) What is the **atomic number** of magnesium?

....

Top Tips: It's sometimes easy to confuse the different parts of an atom. So make sure you learn the differences between protons, neutrons and electrons and where they're found.

Module C4 — The Periodic Table

Atoms

Q5 Choose the correct words to **complete** this paragraph.

element	isotopes	mass	atomic

.... are different atomic forms of the same .... which have the same .... number but a different .... number.

Q6 Below are four different types of atom.

W $\quad ^{12}_{6}C$ X $\quad ^{4}_{2}He$ Y $\quad ^{14}_{6}C$ Z $\quad ^{14}_{7}N$

a) State which of the atoms have the same **mass** number.

Answer: .... and ....

b) State which of the atoms have the same **atomic** number.

Answer: .... and ....

c) State which of the two atoms are **isotopes** of each other.

Answer: .... and ....

Q7 Elements have a **mass number** and an **atomic number**.

a) What does the **mass number** of an element tell you?

....

b) What does the **atomic number** of an element tell you?

....

c) Fill in this table using a periodic table.

Element	Symbol	Mass Number	Number of Protons
Sodium			11
		16	8
Neon			10
	Ca	40	

Module C4 — The Periodic Table

Elements and the Periodic Table

Q1 Choose from these **elements** to answer the following questions.

iodine, nickel, silicon, sodium, radon, krypton, calcium

a) Which two elements are in the same group? .... and ....

b) Name two elements that are in Period 3. .... and ....

c) Name an element in Group 1. ....

d) Name an element with seven electrons in its outer shell. ....

You can use the periodic table to help you for this one.

Q2 Tick the correct boxes to show whether these statements are **true** or **false**.

                                                                                                      True False

a) The periodic table shows the elements in order of ascending **atomic mass**.

b) Columns in the periodic table are called periods.

c) Rows in the periodic table are called groups.

d) Each new period in the periodic table represents another full shell of electrons.

Q3 Circle the **correct words** in these sentences.

a) CO_2 is **a compound / an element**.

b) Fe is **a compound / an element**.

Q4 Elements in the same group **react in a similar way**.

The periodic table will help with this question too.

a) Tick the pairs of elements that would react in a similar way.

    A   potassium and rubidium ☐   C   calcium and oxygen ☐

    B   helium and fluorine ☐   D   calcium and magnesium ☐

b) Fill in the gaps to explain why sodium and potassium react in a similar way with water.

properties	Group 1	outer electrons

Sodium and potassium are both in ....

This means that they both have the same number of ....

This gives them similar ....

Module C4 — The Periodic Table

History of the Periodic Table

Q1 Which of the following statements about **Mendeleev's** Table of Elements are **true** and which are **false**? Tick the correct boxes.

True False

a) Mendeleev arranged the elements in order of increasing atomic mass. ☐ ☐

b) Elements with similar properties appeared in the same rows. ☐ ☐

Q2 Circle the way in which **Döbereiner** chose elements for his **triads**.

The elements had similar properties.   The elements had similar names.   The elements had similar atomic masses.

Q3 Both Newlands and Mendeleev put the elements into a **table**.

Put ticks in the table below to show if each statement is **true** about how they tried to arrange the elements. Some statements are true for both scientists.

	Newlands	Mendeleev
Put the elements in order of relative atomic mass.		
Left gaps for new elements.		
Elements with similar properties were in vertical groups.		
The pattern in the table broke down on the third row.		

Q4 It took a long time for scientists to produce the periodic table that we have today. Draw lines to put these people's ideas on the time line in the **correct order**.

earliest → latest

| Mendeleev created his table of elements. | Döbereiner organised elements into triads. | Newlands put the elements into sets of eight called Newlands' Octaves |

b) Ideas about how to arrange the elements kept changing. Give a reason why.

....

....

Module C4 — The Periodic Table

Electron Shells

Q1 The following statements are **all false**. Write out **corrected versions** of the statements.

a) Protons are found in shells in atoms.

....

b) The outer shells are always filled first.

....

c) Elements in Group 0 have a half full outer shell of electrons.

....

Q2 What is **wrong** with this diagram? Circle the statements.

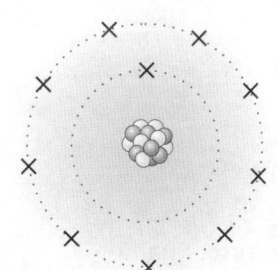

The outer shell contains too many electrons.

The outer shell doesn't contain enough electrons.

There should be two electrons in the inner shell.

There should be eight electrons in the inner shell.

Q3 Write down the **number of electrons** and the **number of occupied shells** for elements with the following electronic structures.

a) **2, 8, 6**   electrons ....   c) **2, 6**   electrons ....

shells ....   shells ....

b) **2**   electrons ....   d) **2, 8, 4**   electrons ....

shells ....   shells ....

Q4 Complete the table with the correct **period**, **group** and **element** for each electronic structure. The first one is done for you.

Electronic structure	Period	Group	Element
2,8,4	3	4	silicon
2,2			
2,3			
2,8,8			

Module C4 — The Periodic Table

Ionic Bonding

Q1 Fill in the gaps in the sentences below by choosing the correct words from the box.

| charged atoms | electrons | ions | attracted to | ionic bond |

a) When a metal and a non-metal combine they form an ....

b) In ionic bonding atoms lose or gain .... to form ....

c) Ions are ....

d) Ions with opposite charges are strongly .... each other.

Q2 Write whether the following are an **atom**, an **ion**, or a **molecule**.

a) Mg^{2+} .... c) O_2 .... e) He ....

b) NO_3^- .... d) H_2O .... f) Na^+ ....

Q3 **Magnesium oxide** is formed from two ions.

a) What name is given to the structure of magnesium oxide? Circle the correct name.

giant ionic lattice   simple irregular lattice   giant irregular lettuce

b) Tick the box to say if the following statements are **true** or **false**.

  True False

i) Magnesium oxide is **not** able to conduct electricity when it is molten.

ii) Magnesium oxide has a higher melting point than sodium chloride.

iii) Magnesium oxide has a very low melting point.

Q4 Mike wants to find out if **sodium chloride** conducts electricity.
He tests it when it's solid, when it's dissolved in water and when it's molten.

Complete the table of results. Some of it has already been filled in for you.

	Conducts electricity?
When solid	
When dissolved in water	✓
When molten	

Module C4 — The Periodic Table

Ions and Ionic Compounds

Q1 Tick the correct boxes to show whether the following statements are **true** or **false**.

		True	False
a)	Ions of metals and non-metals attract one another to form ionic compounds.	☐	☐
b)	Metals form negatively charged ions.	☐	☐
c)	To get a full outer shell, metals usually lose electrons.	☐	☐
d)	Non-metals gain electrons when they form ions.	☐	☐
e)	Atoms form ions because they are more stable when they have full outer shells.	☐	☐
f)	For a non-metal to fill its outer shell, it's easiest for it to gain electrons.	☐	☐
g)	Atoms with 8 electrons in their outer shell have an unstable electronic structure.	☐	☐

Q2 a) Strontium bromide is a **compound** made up of strontium ions (Sr^{2+}) and bromide ions (Br^-). Circle the **formula** of strontium bromide below.

$SrBr$ Sr_2Br $SrBr_2$ Sr_2Br_2

b) Chromium (III) oxide is a compound made up of chromium ions (Cr^{3+}) and oxide ions (O^{2-}). Circle the formula of chromium oxide below.

CrO CrO_2 Cr_2O Cr_2O_3

Q3 Here are some elements and the ions they form:

beryllium, Be^{2+} potassium, K^+ iodine, I^- sulfur, S^{2-}

Make sure the charges on the ions balance.

a) Write down the formulas of four compounds which can be made using these elements.

1. ....   2. ....

3. ....   4. ....

b) State which two elements above are:

i) metals. ....

ii) non-metals. ....

Top Tips: The big thing to remember about ionic compounds is... the charges always **balance**. The oppositely charged ions then strongly attract each other to create an ionic compound. Lovely.

Module C4 — The Periodic Table

Covalent Bonding

Q1 Tick the boxes to show whether each statement is **true** or **false**.

True False

a) Covalent bonding involves sharing electron pairs. ☐ ☐

b) Metals form covalent bonds. ☐ ☐

c) Covalent bonding happens between ions. ☐ ☐

"Oi, give me that electron big nose!"

Q2 Carbon dioxide is a covalently bonded molecule. Complete these sentences by circling the correct word from each pair.

a) Carbon dioxide has a **giant** / **simple** molecular structure.

b) Atoms within covalent molecules are held together by **strong** / **weak** covalent bonds.

c) Carbon dioxide **does** / **doesn't** conduct electricity.

Q3 Choose from the phrases in the boxes to **correctly label** the diagram below.

| weak forces between molecules | strong covalent bonds between atoms |

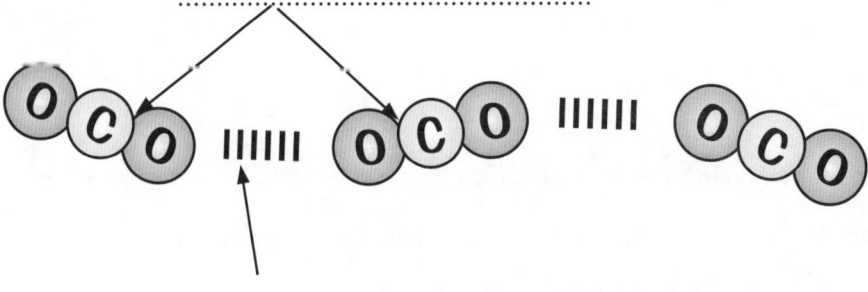

Q4 Circle the following statements about water that are **true**.

Water has a large covalent structure.

The atoms in a water molecule are held together by ionic bonds.

Water has weak intermolecular forces between its molecules.

Pure water does not conduct electricity.

Water has a simple molecular structure.

Top Tips: Don't get covalent bonding mixed up with ionic bonding — there's a big difference between atoms sharing electrons and transferring them.

Module C4 — The Periodic Table

Group 1 — Alkali Metals

Q1 Tick the correct boxes to show whether the statements below are **true** or **false**.

True False

a) Alkali metals have seven electrons in their outer shell. ☐ ☐

b) Caesium is an alkali metal. ☐ ☐

c) Alkali metals are stored in oil to stop them reacting with oxygen and water in the air. ☐ ☐

d) Alkali metals increase in reactivity as you go down the group. ☐ ☐

e) All alkali metals burn with a lilac flame. ☐ ☐

f) Alkali metals are called that because they produce an alkali when they melt. ☐ ☐

Q2 Lithium, sodium and potassium are **alkali metals**.

a) Put **lithium**, **sodium** and **potassium** in order of **increasing** reactivity.

   least reactive ....

   ....

   most reactive ....

b) Explain why alkali metals all have similar properties.

....

....

Q3 Archibald put a piece of **lithium** into a beaker of water.

a) Circle the correct words to answer the questions below.

i) Name the gas that is given off during this reaction.

   oxygen   hydrogen   lithium   nitrogen

ii) LiOH is also formed during this reaction. What is the name of this type of chemical?

   metal oxide   metal hydroxide   metal hydride

   A metal-ox-hide

iii) After the reaction had finished, Archibald tested the pH of the water. Would it be **alkaline**, **acidic** or **neutral**?

   alkaline   acidic   neutral

b) Write the **word equation** for the reaction.

....

Module C4 — The Periodic Table

Group 1 — Alkali Metals

Q4 Alkali metal compounds burn with characteristic **colours** when they're heated.

a) Put these stages (1–4) in order to describe the method of a flame test.

- [ ] Dip a wire loop into a solid sample of the compound to be tested.
- [ ] Record what colour flame is produced.
- [ ] Place the end of the wire loop into a blue Bunsen flame.
- [ ] Dip a wire loop into some acid.

b) Match the alkali metal to its flame test colour.

lithium — red

potassium — yellow / orange

sodium — lilac

Q5 Name the **alkali metal** present in the following:

a) An alkali metal nitrate (found in gunpowder) that produces a lilac flame ....

b) A street lamp that emits an orange light ....

c) Fireworks that produce red flames ....

Q6 **Potassium** will react with water.

a) Write out a word equation for the reaction between potassium and water.

....

b) Use these symbols to write a symbol equation for this reaction.

| 2KOH | 2K | H_2 | $2H_2O$ |

.... + ... → .... + ...

c) Would the reaction of **rubidium** with water be **more** or **less** violent than this reaction?

....

> **Top Tips:** Alkali metals are really reactive elements. In fact, they're so reactive that potassium actually catches fire when it's put in water. Their compounds burn with really distinctive colours as well — make sure you know what these are.

Module C4 — The Periodic Table

Group 7 — Halogens

Q1 Draw lines to match each halogen to its correct **formula**, **description** (at room temperature) and **reactivity**. One has been done for you.

HALOGEN	FORMULA	DESCRIPTION	REACTIVITY
bromine	Cl_2	green gas	least reactive
chlorine	I_2	grey solid	quite reactive
fluorine	Br_2	orange liquid	very reactive
iodine	F_2	yellow gas	most reactive

(fluorine — F_2 — yellow gas — most reactive line shown)

Q2 Draw lines to match each of these uses to the correct halogen.

One of the halogens has two uses from the list and another has none.

- used to sterilise water — chlorine
- used to make pesticides and plastics — iodine
- used to sterilise wounds — bromine

Q3 Tick the correct boxes to say whether these statements are **true** or **false**.

                                        True   False

a) Chlorine gas is made up of molecules which each contain three chlorine atoms. ☐ ☐

b) The halogens react very slowly with alkali metals. ☐ ☐

c) The halogens form metal halides with alkali metals. ☐ ☐

d) A more reactive halogen will displace less reactive halogens from metal halides. ☐ ☐

e) The halogens react in similar ways because they all have seven electrons in their outer shell. ☐ ☐

Q4 **Chlorine** will react with the **alkali metals** and **metal halides**.

a) i) Write the word equation for the reaction between chlorine and the alkali metal **sodium**.

....

ii) Complete the balanced symbol equation below to show the reaction between chlorine and the alkali metal **sodium**.

$$2 \ldots\ldots + Cl_2 \rightarrow 2 \ldots\ldots$$

b) i) Chlorine reacts with the metal halide **sodium bromide** to make **sodium chloride** and **bromine**. Write the word equation for the reaction between chlorine and sodium bromide.

....

ii) Complete the balanced symbol equation below to show this reaction.

$$2\ NaBr + \ldots\ldots \rightarrow 2 \ldots\ldots + Br_2$$

Group 7 — Halogens

Q5 Sodium was reacted with **bromine vapour** using the equipment shown. White crystals of a new solid were formed during the reaction.

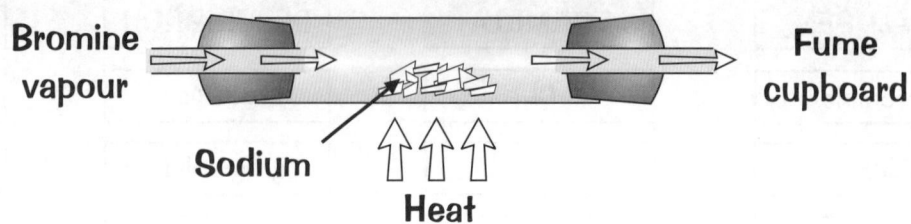

a) Name the white crystals.

    ....

b) Write a word equation for the reaction.

    ....

c) Would the reaction above be **faster** or **slower** than a reaction between sodium and **iodine vapour**?

    ....

d) Explain your answer to part **c)**.

    ....

    ....

Q6 Mrs O'Braid added some **bromine water** to **potassium chloride solution**. She added the same amount to some **potassium iodide solution**. The results are shown in the table.

SOLUTION	RESULT
potassium chloride	no colour change
potassium iodide	colour change

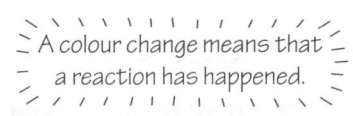

A colour change means that a reaction has happened.

Circle the correct word(s) in each pair to complete the sentences below.

a) i) When bromine water was added to **potassium chloride** solution, the colour **did / didn't** change.

   ii) This was because bromine is **more / less** reactive than chlorine.

   iii) So bromine **displaced / didn't displace** chlorine from the potassium chloride solution.

b) i) When bromine water was added to **potassium iodide** solution, the colour **did / didn't** change.

   ii) This was because bromine is **more / less** reactive than iodine.

   iii) So bromine **displaced / didn't displace** iodine from the potassium iodide solution.

Module C4 — The Periodic Table

Metals

Q1 This diagram shows the **structure** of a metal.

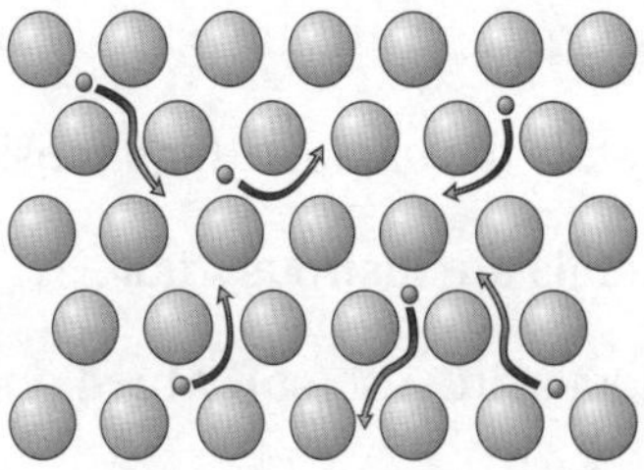

a) What type of bonding does the diagram show?
Circle the correct answer.

ionic   covalent   metallic

b) Tick the box next to the sentence that explains why metals are **good conductors of electricity**.
- [ ] Metals are really poor conductors of heat.
- [ ] Metals have free electrons which can carry electrical current through the metal.
- [ ] The metal atoms can carry current through the metal.

Q2 The table shows the properties of **four elements** found in the periodic table.

ELEMENT	MELTING POINT (°C)	DENSITY (g/cm³)	ELECTRICAL CONDUCTIVITY
A	1084	8.9	Excellent
B	−39	13.6	Very good
C	3500	3.51	Very poor
D	1536	7.87	Very good

a) Which three of the above elements are most likely to be **metals**?

....

b) Explain how you know the other element is **not** a metal.

....

....

Q3 Circle the **correct words** to complete the following sentences about metals.

a) The particles in metals are held together by .... bonds.

weak   strong   disordered

b) This means metals have .... melting and boiling points.

low   high   average

Module C4 — The Periodic Table

Metals

Q4 Circle the correct word in each pair to complete the following sentences.

a) Metals have a **low** / **high** tensile strength.

b) Metals are **lustrous** / **dull**.

c) Metals are also **soft** / **hard** and have **low** / **high** density.

Some metal is heavy.

Q5 This table shows some of the **properties** of four different **metals**.

Metal	Heat Conduction	Cost	Strength	Density
1	average	high	good	very low
2	average	medium	excellent	high
3	excellent	low	good	high
4	low	high	poor	low

Something made of a low density metal will be lighter than if it was made of a high density metal.

Use the information in the table to choose which metal would be **best** for making:

a) Saucepan bases ………… b) Car bodies ………… c) Aeroplanes …………

Q6 **Metals** are used for different things depending on their **properties**.

For each of the uses below, choose the most suitable metal from the list.
Then state one property of the metal that makes it suitable for this purpose.

                       copper   **iron**

a) Structures like bridges.

    Metal ……………………………………

    Property ……………………………………………………………………………………

b) Electrical wiring.

    Metal ……………………………………

    Property ……………………………………………………………………………………

Top Tips: Okay, so metals form weird bonds. How come the electrons can go wandering about like that? Well actually, that's just the kind of question you **don't** need to ask yourself right now. Don't stress about it, just learn the key phrases examiners like — '**sea of free electrons**', etc.

Module C4 — The Periodic Table

Superconductors and Transition Metals

Q1 Use the **periodic table** below, and the one on the inside front cover of this book to help you answer the following questions.

a) On the periodic table above, label the transition metals.

b) Circle any of the following elements that are transition metals.

Ti   zinc   Br   argon   calcium   Na
   copper   Ag

c) Give the **symbols** for the following transition metals:

i) Iron .... ii) Platinum ....

iii) Nickel .... iv) Tungsten ....

d) Give the **names** of the following transition metals:

i) Mn .... ii) Co ....

iii) Y .... iv) Au ....

Q2 Draw lines to match each transition metal to the process it catalyses.

iron — part of the manufacture of margarine

nickel — Haber process

Q3 Tick the boxes to show whether the following statements are **true** or **false**.

a) Really good conductors, like copper, have no electrical resistance.

b) Electrical resistance causes some energy to be wasted as heat.

c) Superconductors have no electrical resistance.

d) At high temperatures some metals can be superconductors.

Module C4 — The Periodic Table

Superconductors and Transition Metals

Q4 Colourful crystals can be made by sprinkling **transition metal compounds** into **sodium silicate solution**.

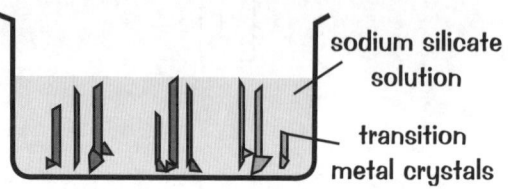

Draw a line between the different transition metal compounds and the colour crystal they would produce.

Q5 Complete the passage below by circling the correct word(s) from each pair.

> The transition metals block is found **at the left / in the middle** of the periodic table. Transition metals generally have **low / high** melting points, high **densities / volatility** and are **good / poor** conductors of heat and electricity. Their compounds are **colourful / shiny** and, like the metals themselves, are often effective **fuels / catalysts**.

Q6 a) What is a **superconductor**? Circle the correct answer.

- A material that has a very high electrical resistance.
- A material that has no electrical resistance.
- A material that can't conduct electricity.

b) Circle **three** possible uses of superconducting wires.

power cables   wire fences   electromagnets   paperclips   electronic circuits   electric heaters

---

Top Tips: Remember — most elements are metals and most metals have similar properties. But don't be a fool and think they're all **identical** — there are lots of little differences which make them useful for different things. Some metals are pretty weird — for example mercury is liquid at room temperature, which means it's not ideal for making cars, spoons, bridges and saucepans.

Module C4 — The Periodic Table

Thermal Decomposition and Precipitation

Q1 Draw lines to match the type of reaction with its description.

thermal decomposition — a substance breaking down into at least two other substances when it's heated

precipitation — two solutions reacting to form an insoluble solid

Q2 Neil heats some **green** copper carbonate, $CuCO_3$. He is left with a **black** solid.

a) How can Neil tell that a reaction has taken place?

....

b) What type of reaction has taken place? ....

c) A gas is made in the reaction. Name this gas.

....

d) Neil tests the gas that's given off in the reaction by bubbling it through **limewater**. Describe what he would see.

....

Q3 Cilla has a solution of an unknown metal ion. To find out what metal ion it is she adds a few drops of **sodium hydroxide** solution. After a while a **blue solid** is left at the bottom.

a) What type of reaction occurred? ....

b) What is the name for the blue solid? Circle the correct answer.

    precipitate   decomposition   coagulate

c) Use **three** of the ions below to complete the table.

    Cu^{2+} Fe^{3+} Fe^{2+} Al^{3+}

Metal ion	Colour of solid formed when sodium hydroxide added to solution
	blue
	grey / green
	orange / brown

Module C4 — The Periodic Table

Water Purity

Q1 Tick the boxes to show whether the following statements are **true** or **false**.

	True	False
a) Aquifers and reservoirs are water resources that are found in the UK.	☐	☐
b) Water from lakes and rivers is not used by industry.	☐	☐
c) Water is an important raw material in industry.	☐	☐
d) The water resources in the UK are unlimited.	☐	☐
e) Water is only used in industry to heat things up.	☐	☐

Q2 Helen's house has **old water pipes**. She's worried about **pollutants** in the tap water.

a) Suggest a type of pollutant that could come from old pipes.

....

b) Helen's water comes from an area with lots of farms. Circle two types of pollutant that could come from farms and could stay in the water after it was purified.

       pesticide   **nitrate**   **particulate**

Q3 Water is **purified** before it reaches our homes.

a) Suggest **two** unwanted substances that purification removes from water.

....

....

b) Draw lines to match the processes to the **order** that they occur and **what they do**.

First	Sedimentation	kills microbes
Second	Chlorination	takes large solid bits out
Third	Filtration	makes small particles clump together and settle so they can be removed

Q4 Explain why it is important to conserve water.

....

....

Module C4 — The Periodic Table

Testing Water Purity

Q1 **Sodium sulfate** reacts with **barium chloride** to form an insoluble solid.

a) What type of reaction is this? Circle the correct answer.

        precipitation   decomposition   purification

b) Complete the word equation for this reaction.

sodium sulfate + barium chloride → barium .... + ...

c) State the **colour** of the solid formed in this reaction.

....

Q2 Sam uses some **silver nitrate solution** to help her identify **halide ions** present in a sample of water.

a) Complete the table to show the colours of the precipitate she could expect for different halide ions.

Ion	Colour of precipitate
	white
bromide	
	yellow

b) Use the words below to complete the word equations showing the reactions between silver nitrate solution and halide ions.

You might have to use the words once, more than once or not at all.

    silver nitrate   sodium nitrate   silver iodide   sodium bromide   sodium chloride

i) silver nitrate + ... → silver chloride + sodium nitrate

ii) silver nitrate + ... → silver bromide + ...

iii) silver nitrate + sodium iodide → .... + ...

Q3 Jukka tests a sample of water from his local duck pond using $AgNO_3$ and $BaCl_2$ solutions. A **white precipitate** forms.

State the **two** ions that could be present in the sample.

1. ....

2. ....

Top Tips: Gah... this seems so much more complicated than it really is. Just make sure you sit down and learn which ions produce which coloured precipitates and how to write out the equations.

Module C4 — The Periodic Table

Mixed Questions — Module C4

Q1 Hydrogen atoms can exist as three **isotopes** — ^1_1H (hydrogen), ^2_1H (deuterium) and ^3_1H (tritium).

a) Circle the correct ending to the sentence:
Isotopes are different forms of the same element that have...

...the same number of protons, but a different number of electrons.

...the same number of neutrons, but a different number of protons.

...the same number of protons, but a different number of neutrons.

b) Which isotope of hydrogen has **one proton** and **two neutrons**?

....

Q2 **Lithium** and **fluorine** are both reactive chemicals.

a) Which group of the periodic table is lithium in?

....

b) i) Describe how lithium behaves if it's put in a beaker of **water**.

....

....

ii) **Sodium** has similar properties to lithium. Explain why.

....

iii) Circle one of the methods below that you could use to test a powdered substance for the presence of lithium.

    precipitation reaction   flame test   bubble it through limewater

c) i) How many electrons does a **lithium atom** have in its outer shell? ....

ii) Circle the answer which explains how lithium **ions**, Li^+, are formed.

    a lithium atom   a lithium atom   a lithium atom
    loses an electron   gains an electron   shares an electron

d) i) Is **fluorine** a metal or a non-metal? Circle the correct answer.   metal   non-metal

ii) How many electrons does a **fluoride ion**, Fl^-, have in its outer shell? ....

e) i) Tick the box next to the statement that best describes **how bonds are formed** between lithium and fluorine to make **lithium fluoride**.

☐ The positive Li^+ ions are attracted to the negative Fl^- ions.

☐ The positive Li^+ ions share electron pairs with the negative Fl^- ions.

☐ The positive Li^+ ions take an electron off the negative Fl^- ions.

ii) What type of bonding is present in lithium fluoride? Circle the appropriate letter.

    A covalent bonding   **B** ionic bonding   **C** metallic bonding

Module C4 — The Periodic Table

Mixed Questions — Module C4

Q3 Group 7 elements all have **similar properties**.

a) What is the name for Group 7 elements? Circle the correct answer.

halogens   alkali metals   noble gases

b) Describe how the **reactivity** of Group 7 elements changes as you go down the group.

....

c) Chlorine is a Group 7 element. It reacts with magnesium to produce **magnesium chloride**.

i) Write a **word equation** for this reaction.

....

ii) Join the following substances to their correct **structure** and fill in the type of **bonding**.

Substance	Structure	Type of Bonding
Magnesium		....
Magnesium chloride		....
Chlorine		....

d) **Bromine** is a Group 7 element with a **simple molecular structure**.

i) What type of bonding binds the bromine atoms together in each molecule? ....

ii) Circle the correct word in each pair to complete the following sentence.

The forces **within / between** bromine molecules are weak

so it takes **little / lots of** energy to separate them.

iii) **Iodine** also has a simple molecular structure. State whether iodine is able to conduct electricity.

....

e) Chlorine gas (Cl_2) can react with potassium bromide (KBr) to form bromine (Br_2) and potassium chloride (KCl). Write a balanced symbol equation for this reaction.

....

Module C4 — The Periodic Table

Static Electricity

Q1 Circle the pairs of charges that would attract each other and underline those that would repel.

positive and positive   positive and negative   negative and positive   negative and negative

Q2 Fill in the gaps in these sentences with the words below.

electrons	positive	static	insulating	negative

.... electricity can build up when two .... materials are rubbed together. The .... move from one material onto the other. This leaves a .... charge on one of the materials and a .... charge on the other.

Q3 Tick the boxes to show whether the following statements are **true** or **false**.

	True	False
a) Electrons are negatively charged particles.	☐	☐
b) Areas of positive charge are caused by the movement of positive charges.	☐	☐
c) Negatively charged areas occur because electrons are attracted to each other.	☐	☐

Q4 The sentences below are wrong. Write out a **correct** version for each.

a) An insulating rod becomes negatively charged when rubbed with a duster because it loses electrons.

....

....

b) A charged duster will repel dust when placed near a dusty surface.

....

....

c) Like charges attract each other.

....

....

More on Static Electricity

Q1 A library had to be closed after **synthetic carpets** were fitted.
People complained of **electric shocks** when they touched the **metal** handrail on the stairs.

Why did people get electric shocks? Circle the letter of the correct explanation below.

- **A** — Synthetic carpets are always charged. When the people touched the metal rail, this charge flowed through them from the carpet to the rail.

- **B** — They became charged as their shoes rubbed against the carpet. When they touched the metal rail the charge flowed to earth.

- **C** — Synthetic carpets are good conductors. The people were feeling the electric current flowing through the carpet.

Q2 Choose from the words below to complete the passage.

fuel   explosion   metal   paper rollers   grain chutes   sparks

Static electricity can be dangerous when refuelling cars. If too much static builds up, there might be .... which could set fire to the ....
This could lead to an .... To prevent this happening, the nozzle is made of .... so the charge is conducted away. There are similar safety problems with .... and ....

Q3 Three friends are talking about some of the effects of **static electricity**.

Lisa: Why do you sometimes get lightning during a storm?

Tim: Why do my clothes cling together after they've been tumble dried?

Sara: Why is the TV screen always dusty — my mum cleans it all the time?

Answer their questions in terms of **charges**.

Lisa: ....
....

Sara: ....
....

Tim: ....
....

Module P4 — Radiation for Life

Uses of Static Electricity

Q1 Complete this paragraph by choosing words from the list below.

| precipitator | plates | charge | particles | positive | attracted | fall off |

Smoke contains tiny .... The smoke can be cleaned up with a dust .... One sort uses a wire grid to give the particles a negative .... They then pass between two metal .... which have a .... charge. The particles are .... to the plates. The plates are hit with a hammer so the particles ....

Q2 A **defibrillator** is a machine used by doctors to give **electric shocks**.

a) What are defibrillators used for? Circle the answer.

To break down kidney stones.   To treat cancer.

To restart the heart.

b) Circle the correct word in each pair to describe how the patient is given an electric shock.

Two charged **paddles** / **oars**, which are connected to a **power** / **water** supply, are placed firmly on the patient's **head** / **chest**. The **charge** / **water** then passes through the patient.

Q3 The diagram shows an **electrostatic** paint sprayer.

a) How do the drops of paint become **charged**?
....

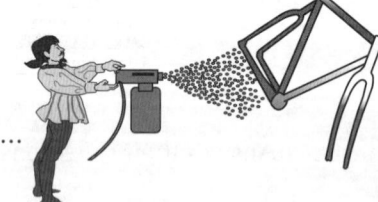

b) Why does this help produce a **fine spray**?
....

c) Explain how the paint drops are **attracted** to the object being sprayed.
....

d) Explain why the object being painted doesn't need to be **turned** round while it is being sprayed.
....

Module P4 — Radiation for Life

Charge and Resistance

Q1 Use the words below to complete the passage.
You may need to use some words **more than once**.

| protons | charge | resistance | voltage | increase | reduce |

Current is the flow of .... around a circuit. The driving force that pushes

the current through a component is the .... Resistance tends to

.... the flow. To increase the current in a circuit you can

.... the resistance or .... the voltage.

Q2 Draw lines to connect the **quantities** with their **units** and unit **symbols**.

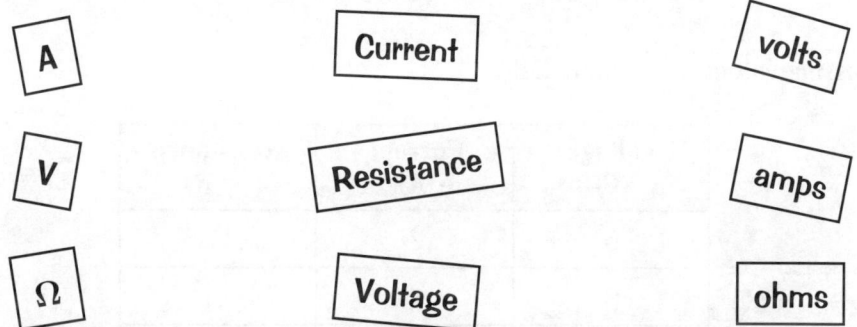

Q3 The flow of electricity in circuits is a bit like the flow of **water in pipes**.

a) Draw lines to connect the labelled parts of a water circuit
with the matching parts of an electrical circuit.

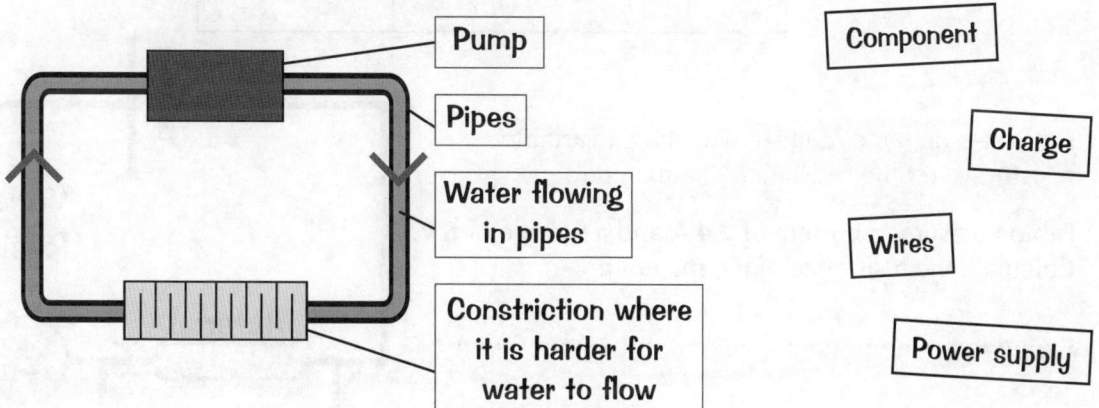

b) The pump in the water circuit is turned up.
What action would have the same effect in an electrical circuit? Circle the correct answer.

Increasing the voltage of the power supply   Increasing the resistance of the power supply

Top Tips: Anything that slows the flow of charge down has resistance. Slowing the charge decreases the current. Make sure you get the hang of this and you'll be scooping up the marks like a small child let loose at the pick and mix counter. Enjoy.

Module P4 — Radiation for Life

Charge and Resistance

Q4 Complete these sentences by **circling** the correct word from each pair.

a) Increasing the voltage **increases / decreases** the current that flows, if the resistance is constant.

b) If the voltage is constant, to increase the current you need to **increase / decrease** the resistance.

c) If the resistance is increased, **more / less** current will flow if the voltage is constant.

Q5 Tick the boxes to show whether these statements are **true** or **false**.

	True	False
A variable resistor is used to alter the current passing through a circuit.	☐	☐
Longer wires have more resistance than shorter wires.	☐	☐
Thinner wires have less resistance than thicker wires.	☐	☐

Q6 Fill in the **missing values** in the table below.

Resistance = Voltage ÷ Current

Voltage (V)	Current (A)	Resistance (Ω)
6	2	
8	4	
9	3	
4	8	
2	0.5	
1	0.5	

Q7 Fabio sets up the circuit shown using a **variable resistor** to test the resistance of a material.

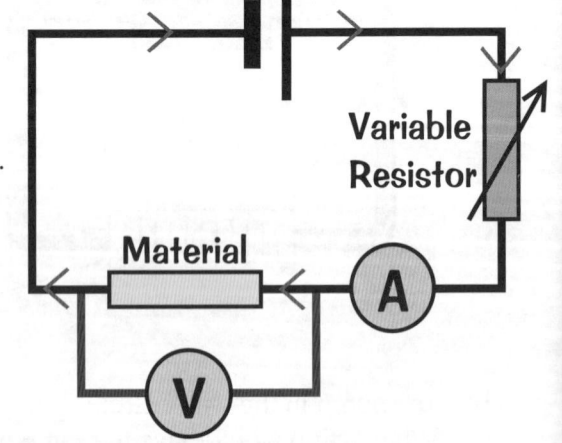

a) Fabio measures a current of **2.4 A** and a voltage of **6 V**. Calculate the resistance of the material.

....

....

....

b) How would Fabio use the variable resistor to help get a **reliable** result from his experiment?

....

....

....

Module P4 — Radiation for Life

Plugs, Fuses and Power

Q1 Circle the right words in each pair below to describe the main difference between a **fuse** and a **circuit breaker**.

   A **fuse / circuit breaker** can be reset and used again.

   Fuses / Circuit breakers melt when they 'blow' and have to be replaced.

Q2 Put these events in the **correct order** to describe what happens when a **fault** occurs in an earthed kettle. Label the events from 1 to 4.

- [ ] The circuit is broken so the current stops flowing.
- [ ] The big current melts the fuse.
- [ ] A big current flows out through the earth wire.
- [ ] A fault allows the live wire to touch the metal case.

Q3 Draw lines to match each of the wires found in a **plug** with its colour and description.

Neutral	Green and yellow	Carries the high voltage
Live	Blue	Completes the circuit
Earth	Brown	A safety wire

Q4 A '**double insulated**' hairdryer uses a current of **3.7 A**.

Why does the hairdryer **not** need an **earth wire**?
Circle the correct answer.

A — Only appliances with a current higher than 5 A need an earth wire.

B — Double insulated appliances never get faults.

C — The case is not made of metal so it can never become live.

Module P4 — Radiation for Life

Plugs, Fuses and Power

Q5 Tom is making **toast** and **tea** for breakfast. His house has a **230 V** mains electricity supply.

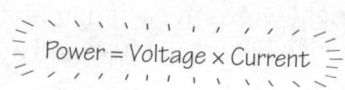

Power = Voltage × Current

a) Tom's toaster draws **4 A** of current. Calculate the power rating of his toaster.

....

....

b) Tom puts on the kettle to make tea. The kettle draws **7.5 A** of current. Calculate the power rating of his kettle.

....

....

c) Tom's toaster has a metal case. His kettle has a plastic case. Which one needs an earth wire? Circle the right answer.

| The toaster | The kettle | Both the toaster and the kettle |

Q6 Calculate the power ratings of the appliances to complete the table below.

Appliance	Voltage (V)	Current (A)	Power (W)
A	9	3	
B	230	5	
C	12	0.5	
D	230	2.9	
E	9	0.3	
F	230	8.5	

Top Tips: I'm not going to lie — there's a lot of stuff to learn about using electricity in the home. But the good news is that learning about plugs, fuses, and the power ratings of your appliances will not only come in useful in the exams, it will be mighty handy at home too. So next time a blown fuse cuts out the power while you're making a brew, amaze your family with your expert knowledge. Then sit back and let someone else do the tricky job of actually changing the fuse...

Module P4 — Radiation for Life

Ultrasound Treatments and Scans

Q1 Draw lines to match up the two parts of each of the following statements.

Ultrasound waves have...

Ultrasound is...

One wavelength is...

... the distance between two compressions of a wave.

... frequencies greater than 20 000 Hz.

... sound beyond the range of human hearing.

Q2 **Ultrasound** is a type of sound wave.

a) What type of wave are sound waves? Circle the correct answer.

longitudinal   transverse

b) Use the words below to label the diagram of a sound wave.

rarefactions   compressions   wavelength

c) i) What is the **frequency** of a wave?

....

ii) Circle the correct word to complete the following sentence:

A high frequency sound wave will have a **higher** / **lower** pitch than a lower frequency sound wave.

d) When sound waves travel through a material they produce **compressions** and **rarefactions**. What are compressions and rarefactions?

Compressions: ....

....

Rarefactions: ....

....

Module P4 — Radiation for Life

Radioactive Decay and Background Radiation

Q1 Draw lines to match the type of radiation with its description.

Alpha — An electromagnetic wave

Beta — A helium nucleus

Gamma — A fast moving electron

Q2 Tick the boxes to show whether the statements are **true** or **false**.

	True	False
a) We can predict when an unstable atom will decay.	☐	☐
b) An alpha particle is made up of two protons and two neutrons.	☐	☐
c) Radiation is emitted by an unstable nucleus.	☐	☐
d) All atoms emit radiation all the time.	☐	☐
e) An unstable nucleus will decay at random.	☐	☐
f) An unstable nucleus will not decay naturally — you have to do something to it to make it decay.	☐	☐
g) All background radiation comes from man-made sources.	☐	☐
h) The level of background radiation is the same wherever you go.	☐	☐

Q3 There is a low level of background radiation all around us.

a) Write down **three** sources of background radiation.

1. ....
2. ....
3. ....

b) In the following situations, would you expect the background radiation to be **higher** or **lower** than average? Explain your answers.

i) Flying in an aeroplane. ....

....

ii) Going down into a mine. ....

....

Module P4 — Radiation for Life

Radioactivity and Half-Life

Q1 Tick the boxes to show whether the following statements are **true** or **false**.

                                                                                                                           True   False

    a) The number of radioactive nuclei in a sample always stays the same.

    b) Radioactive materials decay at different rates.

Q2 Complete the passage using the words given below.

> zero   time   activity   halve   radiation   decreases
>
> The radioactivity of a sample always .... over time.
>
> Each time a decay happens, ... is emitted.
>
> The half-life is the .... taken for the
>
> .... of a radioactive sample to ....
>
> The activity of a sample never reaches ....

Q3 The half-life of uranium-238 is **4500 million years**. The half-life of carbon-14 is **5730 years**.

If you start with a sample of each element and the two samples have equal activity, which will lose its radioactivity more **quickly**? Circle the correct answer.

        uranium-238   carbon-14

Q4 The graph below shows how the radioactivity of sample X varied with time.

    a) What was the radioactivity of sample X after 10 minutes?

    ....

    b) What happened to the radioactivity of sample X over time?

    ....

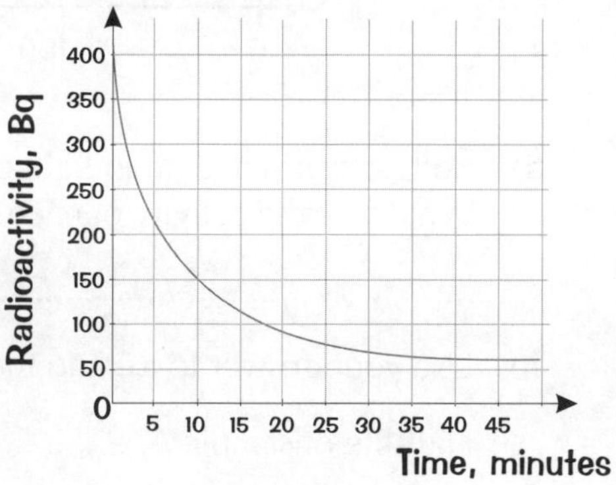

    c) Complete the sentence below.

    Radioactivity is measured by the number of .... **per second.**

Module P4 — Radiation for Life

Radioactivity and Half-Life

Q5   The half-life of strontium-90 is **29 years**.

a)   What will have happened to the activity of a sample of strontium-90 in 29 years' time?

....

b)   A sample of strontium-90 has an activity of **1000 Bq**.
What would you expect the activity of the sample to be after **87 years**?   *Work out the number of half-lives in 87 years first.*

....

....

....

Q6   The graph shows how the **activity** of two radioactive samples, A and B, **changed over time**.

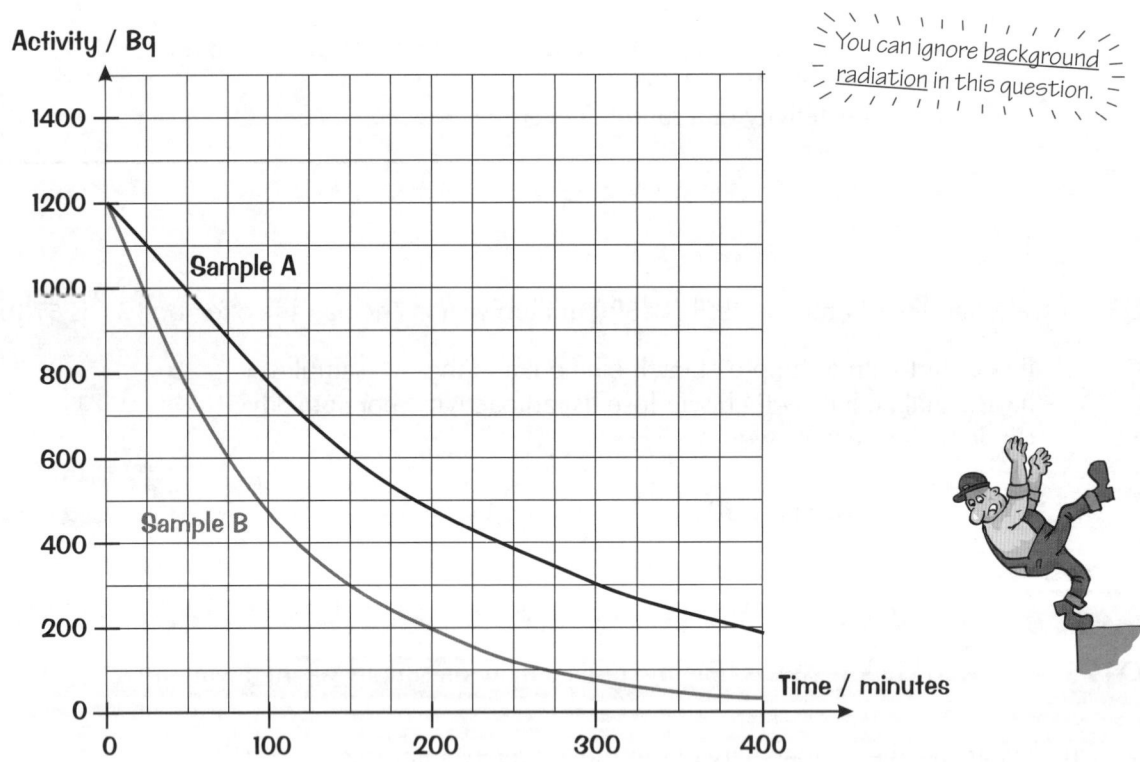

You can ignore background radiation in this question.

a)   Both samples had an initial activity of 1200 Bq.
What was the activity of each sample after **one** of their half-lives?

....

b)   Use your answer to **a)**, and the graph, to **estimate the half-life** of each sample.

Half-life of sample A: ....

Half-life of sample B: ....

Module P4 — Radiation for Life

Ionising Radiation

Q1 Circle the correct word from each pair to compete the sentences below.

a) X-rays and gamma rays are both types of **electromagnetic** / **sound** wave.

b) X-rays and gamma rays are produced in **the same way** / **different ways**.

c) X-rays and gamma rays have **very different** / **similar** wavelengths.

Q2 Use the words in the list below to complete the paragraph.

ionisation	nuclear	molecules	cells	cancer	kill

When X-rays and ……………………… radiation enter ……………………… in the body they

may interact with ……………………… and cause ……………………… .

Radiation can cause ……………………… or ……………………… cells completely.

Q3 The three different types of **nuclear radiation** can all be dangerous.

a) Which **two** types of radiation can pass into the human body from outside? Circle the correct answers.

    alpha   beta   gamma

b) i) Which type of radiation is usually most dangerous if it's inhaled or swallowed?

……………………………………………………………………………………………………

ii) What effects can this type of radiation have on the human body?
Circle **all** the correct answers below.

It can ionise molecules in cells.	It can make you explode.
It can kill cells.	It can break bones.
It can cause bruises.	It can cause cancer.	It can damage cells.

Top Tips: No doubt about it — there is an awful lot to learn about ionising radiation. You need to know what it is, what it can do, and a bit about the different types. So, just for you, there's a whole other page of questions on ionising radiation coming right up, so you can get all the practice you need. It's okay, you don't have to thank me. Just make sure you know your alphas from your X-rays.

Module P4 — Radiation for Life

Ionising Radiation

Q4 X-ray 'photographs' of hospital patients can be taken to see if they have any **broken bones**.

a) What name is given to a hospital worker who takes X-rays?

....

b) As well as the patient, the hospital worker will also be exposed to X-rays.
Give **two** ways they can minimise the amount of radiation they're exposed to.

1. ....

2. ....

c) i) Circle the correct words to complete the following sentences.

The **thicker** / **thinner** a material is, the more X-rays it will absorb.
The denser a material is, the **more** / **fewer** X-rays it will absorb.

ii) The sentences below describe stages in the process of taking an X-ray image.
Draw lines to match the start of each sentence with the correct ending.

The X-rays pass easily...	...forms the X-ray image.
When the X-rays hit bone under the flesh...	...so they appear white on an X-ray image.
The different amount of X-rays absorbed...	...through the patient's flesh.
A lot of X-rays are absorbed by bones...	...most of them are absorbed.

Q5 Barry and Paul are talking about **ionisation**.

Barry: Ionisation makes particles radioactive because it affects the number of neutrons.

Paul: Ionisation affects the number of electrons a particle has.

a) Who is right? Circle the correct answer.

Barry   Paul

b) Briefly explain what happens during ionisation.

....

....

Module P4 — Radiation for Life

Medical Uses of Radiation

Q1 Complete the following paragraph on **radiotherapy** using the words provided.

| ill | normal | kill | carefully | cancer | radiotherapy |

High doses of gamma radiation will .... living cells. Because of this,

gamma radiation is used to treat .... This is called ....

Gamma rays are directed .... on the tumour.

Damage to .... cells can make the patient feel very ....

Q2 Iodine-123 is commonly used as a **tracer** in medicine.

a) The thyroid gland normally **absorbs** iodine.
Number the steps below 1-5 to describe how iodine-123 is used to detect whether the thyroid gland is working properly. One has been done for you.

[ ] The iodine-123 gives out gamma rays from the thyroid gland.
[1] The patient is injected with iodine-123.
[ ] A detector outside the body picks up the gamma rays.
[ ] The iodine-123 is absorbed by the thyroid gland.
[ ] The detected gamma rays show up any problems in the thyroid gland.

b) Give **one** reason, other than safety, why alpha emitters cannot be used as tracers.

....

Q3 The table shows the **properties** of **three** radioactive materials called radioisotopes.

Radioisotope	Half-life
technetium-99m	6 hours
phosphorus-32	14 days
cobalt-60	5 years

a) Which radioisotope would be best to use as a **medical tracer**? Circle the answer.

technetium-99m   phosphorus-32   cobalt-60

b) Explain your answer to part **a)**.

....

....

Module P4 — Radiation for Life

Other Uses of Radiation

Q1 Radioactivity can be used to help **date rocks** and other old materials. Circle the letter(s) next to any true statements below.

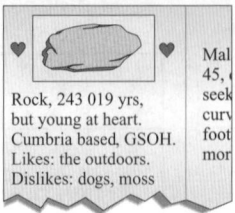

- A Rocks formed more than 1000 years old are not radioactive.

- B The amount of a radioactive material in a rock sample can be measured. The age of the rock can be found using the half-life of that material.

- C Radioactive carbon can be used to date old materials.

Q2 The following sentences explain how a **smoke detector** works, but they are in the wrong order.

Put them in order by labelling them 1 (first) to 6 (last).

- [ ] The current is reduced because there is less ionisation of the air particles.
- [1] The radioactive source emits alpha particles.
- [ ] A current flows inside the detector — the alarm stays off.
- [ ] The alarm sounds.
- [ ] The air inside the detector is ionised by the alpha particles.
- [ ] A fire starts and the alpha radiation hits the smoke particles instead of the air.

Q3 An oil company knows that its pipeline is **leaking** somewhere between points B and E. To find the leak, they plan to inject a source of radiation into the pipeline. They will then pass a sensor along the surface above the pipeline to detect where radiation is escaping.

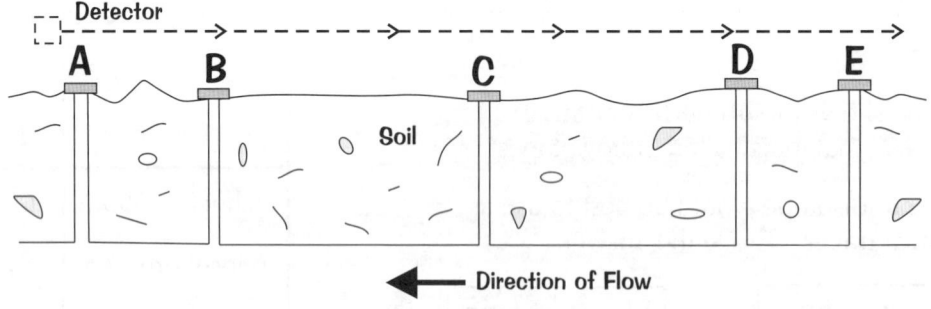

a) What **type** of radioactive source should they **not** use? Circle the correct answer.

alpha   beta   gamma

b) At which **point** (A-E) should they inject the radioactive material? Explain your answer.

....

....

Nuclear Power

Q1 a) Tick the correct boxes to show whether the following statements are **true** or **false**.

True False

i) Nuclear power stations are powered by burning fossil fuels. ☐ ☐

ii) Nuclear power stations do not produce any waste products. ☐ ☐

iii) The reaction in a nuclear reactor is called fission. ☐ ☐

iv) A nuclear bomb is a fission chain reaction that has gone out of control. ☐ ☐

b) Write out a correct version of any false statements in part **a)** below.

....

....

....

....

Q2 Choose from the following words to complete the passage.

> turbine   electricity   uranium   water   steam   generator   heat

Inside a nuclear reactor, ... atoms split and release

.... energy. This energy is used to turn ....

into ....

The steam then turns a ...., which in turn drives a

.................................., producing ....

Q3 The sentences below describe how a nuclear fission **chain reaction** occurs, starting with a single **uranium** atom absorbing a **neutron**. **Number** them 1-4 in the correct order. One has been done for you.

☐ If the neutrons collide with other atoms, these can also split.

☐ More neutrons and more energy are produced.

[1] The uranium atom absorbs the neutron, becomes unstable, and splits up.

☐ Two smaller atoms, two or three neutrons and lots of energy are produced.

Module P4 — Radiation for Life

Nuclear Power

Q4 Materials placed in a nuclear reactor can become **radioactive**. Circle the letter of the statement below that explains **why**.

A — Materials placed in a nuclear reactor will get ionised. Ionisation makes some materials radioactive.

B — Materials placed in a nuclear reactor will absorb neutrons. This makes some materials become radioactive.

C — The temperature in a nuclear reactor gets very high. This makes some materials become radioactive.

Q5 Three friends are discussing **nuclear power**.

Jan says: "Once a nuclear chain reaction starts, it always ends up in a nuclear explosion."

Sophia says: "A nuclear reactor is one way of releasing heat to make steam."

Rafiq says: "There are some serious problems with using nuclear power."

Circle the word below to say whether each is right or wrong, and explain why.

a) Jan is **right** / **wrong** because ....

....

b) Sophia is **right** / **wrong** because ....

....

c) Rafiq is **right** / **wrong** because ....

....

Top Tips: The key thing with nuclear power is to remember what goes on in the reactor. It's really just one big nuclear kettle. A controlled chain reaction is set up and releases heat, which is used to heat water and produce steam. After that it's just like almost all power stations — the steam turns a turbine which turns a generator which makes electricity, which makes cups of tea galore.

Module P4 — Radiation for Life

Nuclear Fusion

Q1 Tick the boxes to show whether the following statements are **true** or **false**.   True   False

a) Nuclear fusion involves small nuclei joining together.

b) For the same mass, nuclear fusion releases more energy than nuclear fission.

c) Fusion reactors produce lots of radioactive waste.

d) Only a few experimental fusion reactors are generating electricity.

Q2 Nuclear fusion releases **energy**.

a) i) What **condition** is needed for nuclear fusion to take place? Circle the answer.

　　a really low temperature　　　　　a vacuum　　　　　a really high temperature

ii) Explain why this makes fusion reactors extremely **hard to build**.

　..

　..

b) List **two** things that are **shared** by international groups carrying out fusion power research.

1. ....

2. ....

Professor Box was always keen to share his collection of old model cars with other scientists.

Q3 In 1989, two scientists claimed to have released energy through **cold fusion**.

a) What is meant by **cold fusion**? Circle the correct words to complete the answer.

| Cold fusion is a nuclear fusion reaction that can work at **–10 °C / room temperature**. |

b) Why were the cold fusion data and experiments **shared** with other scientists? Circle the letter next to the correct answer.

A — So that other scientists could repeat the experiments.

B — To stop other scientists making money from the cold fusion experiments.

C — So that other scientists didn't need to do any more experiments on cold fusion.

c) Explain why most scientists **didn't accept** the idea of cold fusion.

....

....

Module P4 — Radiation for Life

Mixed Questions — Module P4

Q1 The diagram shows an aircraft being refuelled. **No safety precautions** have been taken.

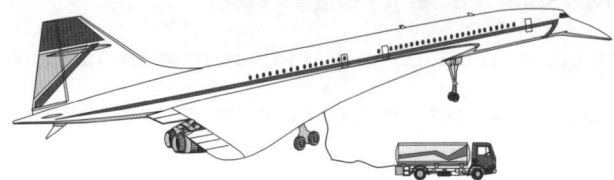

a) i) Explain how static electricity could cause an explosion in this situation.

....

....

ii) Give **one** other situation where static electricity could cause explosions.

....

b) The aircraft needs a new lick of paint. Circle the correct words in the passage below to describe how static electricity could be used to **spray paint** the aircraft.

> The aircraft and spray gun are given **opposite / the same** charges. The paint has
> **an opposite charge to / the same charge as** the gun and is **repelled by / attracted to**
> all parts of the aircraft equally. All the paint drops **repel / attract** one another as
> the paint is being sprayed, giving the aircraft a fine, even coat of paint.

c) Passengers flying on aircraft are exposed to a higher level of background radiation than on the ground. What causes this higher level of background radiation? Circle the answer.

   radioactive waste   rocks   cosmic rays

Q2 Ultrasound is used in **hospitals**.

Hint: ultrasound has a high frequency.

a) What is ultrasound? Circle the correct answer.

   a very loud sound   a very high pitched sound   a very low pitched sound

b) Give **two** ways that ultrasound can be used to **measure or see things** inside the body.

   1. ....

   2. ....

c) Give **one** example of how ultrasound can be used instead of **surgery**.

....

Module P4 — Radiation for Life

Mixed Questions — Module P4

Q3 An electric kettle with a metal case has a plate on the bottom that says "**230 V, 2.3 kW, 10 A**".

a) You have fuses rated at **3 A**, **5 A** and **13 A** available.

The fuse rating is the size of the current that will blow the fuse.

i) Which fuse would you fit in the plug for this kettle? ....

ii) The fuse is connected to the wire that carries the high voltage. Which wire is this? Circle the correct answer.

☐ Live   ☐ Neutral

iii) What colour is this wire?

....

iv) Explain how the fuse prevents a fire if the kettle gets a fault.

....

....

b) The plug also contains an **earth wire**.

i) What colour is this wire?

....

ii) What is the purpose of this wire? Tick the box next to the correct answer.

☐ To complete the electrical circuit.

☐ To stop the appliance becoming live.

☐ To carry the high voltage.

Q4 Paul wants to set the mood for his date with some romantic lighting. He dims the lights using a dimmer switch which uses a **variable resistor**.

I can still see your face...

a) Circle the right word to show whether Paul would need to **increase** or **decrease** the resistance to:

The bigger the current, the brighter the lights.

i) brighten the lights: **increase / decrease**

ii) dim the lights: **increase / decrease**

b) Paul shows off to his date by taking some current and resistance readings with the dimmer switch in three different positions. The voltage is **230 V**. Complete the table.

c) In which position (1-3) will the lights be the brightest?

....

Position	Resistance	Current
1		4.6 A
2		2.3 A
3		9.2 A

Module P4 — Radiation for Life

Mixed Questions — Module P4

Q5 Nuclear radiation is used in many hospital treatments.

a) Which type of radiation would **not** be used as a tracer in the body?
   Give a reason for your answer.

   ....

   ....

b) The activity of most substances used as tracers decreases **quickly**.
   Explain why the radioactivity of **any** radioactive substance decreases over time.

   ....

   ....

c) Gamma sources are used in **cancer treatment**.

   i) Explain how gamma radiation kills cancer cells.

   ....

   ....

   ii) Explain why patients often feel worse rather than better while having this treatment.

   ....

d) What type of nuclear radiation is used to sterilise surgical equipment?

   ....

Q6 Many nuclear power stations use **uranium** to generate electricity.

a) Name the type of reaction that takes place in the nuclear reactor.

   ....

b) What would happen if this reaction got out of control?

   ....

c) Describe how heat from the nuclear reactor is used to generate electricity.

   ....

   ....

d) Many precautions are taken to protect workers at nuclear power stations from radiation.
   Why is nuclear radiation dangerous?

   ....

Module P4 — Radiation for Life